Women's W

A Woman's Place

1974-1999

A celebration of women's lives in Brighton over the last 25 years

A Woman's Place: A celebration of women's lives in Brighton over the last 25 years

Published by **Women's Words**, Brighton
March 1999

This collection copyright © Women's Words 1999
(Copyright © in each contribution held by the individual contributors 1999)

The right of Women's Words to be identified as the author of this work has been asserted by them in accordance with the Copyright, Designs and Patents Act, 1988

A catalogue record of this book is available from the British Library

ISBN 1 874548 30 7

Printed by Digaprint, Brighton, East Sussex
Cover printed by Delta Press, Hove, East Sussex

Front cover: (L–R)
Norma Binnie,
The Counihan Sisters,
Rosemary Lovatt,
Sue Winter
Main photograph:
Hillary Katzenell

Photographs © Lynne Fox (unless credited otherwise)

Design by Wordsmith

Contents

Foreword 4

Introduction 5

The Four Demands 6

25 years of important dates for women 8

The Interviews

Alanna	12	Julia Reddaway	64
Betty Walshe	15	Linda Pointing	67
Counihan Sisters	22	Liz Williams	72
Debbie Harris	26	Michelle Pooley	74
Erica Mackenzie	29	Molly Wadey	78
Erica Smith	31	Nic Fryer	81
Helen Zahavi	36	Norma Binnie	85
Hillary Katzenell	38	Pat	90
Jackie Cairns	41	Polly Marshall	92
Jane	43	Rosemary Lovatt	95
Jean Hopkins	47	Sue Winter	98
Jen Murray	51	Tanya Levene	102
Joyce Edmond-Smith	54	Vicki Brown	106
Judy Richards	57		

Brighton Women's Centre 108

Brighton Oasis Project 112

Launch Project 114

Toy Box Creche 115

Women's Refuge Project 116

Quotes from Women's Centre workers and users 118

About Women's Words 122

Foreword

The publication of this book is an opportunity to look back at women's lives in Brighton over the past twenty-five years. It coincides with the 25th anniversary of the establishment of Brighton Women's Centre.

Within these pages you will find some of the women who helped to set up the Centre, who were there at the very beginning. The book also highlights other organisations and projects which developed, in part, from the Women's Centre, all of which have continued to thrive, and provide essential services for women in Brighton.

The main contributors, the women interviewed, have freely given their memories of certain events in their lives so you, the reader, can share and perhaps recognise some of the feelings expressed.

This project has been undertaken solely by volunteers, who felt it was important to give women the opportunity to talk about their lives and achievements in Brighton. During the past eighteen months, at least 3000 hours of time has been spent, all unpaid, to ensure that this book would be published.

A Woman's Place should be viewed as a living testament to women in Brighton. The women who have worked tirelessly to make this possible should be proud of this book.

Rosemary Lovatt

Introduction

A Woman's Place is a fascinating journey into certain areas of women's lives, a record of the uncharted and diverse activities conducted by women in Brighton. We decided to use oral history techniques to record this journey, as it provides a living record of the way women remember their lives. Oral history also offers us an alternative method of recording history which might not otherwise be documented. This is particularly important for women as, traditionally, mainstream history has often neglected the significance and relevance of documenting women's life stories.

This project has been a difficult process as most of us involved had no experience of putting a book together. Over forty women were interviewed on tape and once completed had to be transcribed (an incredibly lengthy process!). The core of the book draws on the actual words of more than thirty women with extracts from the Women's Centre diaries and page dedications running alongside. It includes a brief history of Brighton Women's Centre, snapshots of services that have been connected with the Centre and an overview of significant events for women in the past twenty-five years. We had to edit the transcripts in order to produce the book, selecting certain parts with the intention of presenting a diversity of women and their experiences. However, it should be mentioned that, *A Woman's Place* is by no means intended to be a comprehensive view of women and their experiences; it is simply a cross-section of the women who were interviewed.

The majority of this project has been funded by individual women, through the giving of their labour, from donations of cash and equipment and through the sponsorship of dedication pages in the book. We gratefully acknowledge financial support from the Hedgecock Bequest and Brighton Women's Centre. To all those people who have supported the project, we thank you.

We also respectfully thank the Brighton Women's Liberation group who met regularly during the 60s and 70s for the title of this book, as it was one they used for their early publications.

Women's Words are delighted to have produced and published this book. We hope that you enjoy it.

Women's Words Project Team
March 1999

The Four Demands

The first Women's Liberation Movement National Conference was held in Oxford in 1970, it was here that it was agreed that the movement should press for four minimum demands.

1. equal pay for equal work
2. equal job and educational opportunities
3. free contraception and abortion on demand
4. free twenty four hour childcare facilities.

At the conference in Edinburgh in 1974 two more demands were added:

5. legal and financial independence for women
6. and end to discrimination against lesbians and the right of all women to our own self defined sexuality

and at Birmingham in 1978

7. freedom from intimidation, violence and sexual coercion.

It was in this heady feeling of sisterhood that the Brighton Women's Centre was first established in 1974. Women formed consciousness-raising groups, where groups of women discussed their lives, supporting and re-evaluating their relationships with men, other women and society.

But how much have we achieved in the last century? The vote, the right to work – even after marriage, to get a mortgage or loan without having to get a man's permission, divorce is easier, access to abortion, contraceptives, equal opportunities in the work place and for those who can afford it, a university education.

Fifty years ago women studied at Cambridge, but as they were not members of the university, they weren't allowed to wear gowns and were not entitled to received their degrees. In 1998 one thousand women finally returned to Cambridge for a ceremony that at last recognised them.

In 1998 the average woman still earned 20% less than the average man. Abortion is now available on the NHS, but more women choose to pay privately, and the decision whether a woman can have an abortion is not solely hers, but rests with two doctors, often male; perhaps a legacy from the 1960s when there was a 20% limit imposed on female candidates applying to do medical degrees.

Positive discrimination in favour of women to address these imbalances is illegal, although men are still reaping the benefits of positive discrimination in favour of them. In the mid 1950s quotas were imposed on grammar schools because too many girls were passing the 11 plus – without the quota two-thirds of the places at grammar schools would have been filled by girls.

The Sex Discrimination Act does not stretch to the 'old boys networks', which women are still excluded from and more men have successfully used the Act than women.

But like most women I wouldn't swap to being a man even for a moment.

Women are consistently achieving high marks in education, we are multi-talented, with good verbal reasoning and communication skills – all essential in the changing workforce. Women account for 54% of all newly qualified solicitors – so we should see more and more women in the upper echelons of the business and political worlds.

If men have set the standards, we are surpassing them – but I predict that before all this can have any real impact we will see positive discrimination in favour of men, if women ever threaten to tip the balance in their favour.

A world where only 3 high court judges are male, where the average man earns 20% less than the average women, where the Houses of Parliament are dominated by women – the thought is preposterous, after all that really wouldn't be fair!

Kelle Kingsley

25 years of important dates for Women

1974

September: Brighton Women's Centre opens in Buckingham Road

Women can now use 'Ms' on official documents

Contraceptives available free on the NHS

1975

First International Women's Day

National Women's Aid Federation formed

United Nations launches the 'Decade for Women'

Margaret Thatcher elected as leader of the Conservative party

Sex Discrimination act piloted through by Nancy Seear and becomes law on 29 December 1975

Mr Andrew Bowden, MP for Kemp Town is a vehement opponent of the Abortion Act. He is reported in the Evening Argus as saying 'Abortion is the deliberate and cold-blooded destruction of human life already created'

1976

Equal Pay Act passed in 1970 is finally implemented

First Rape Crisis centre opens

Angela Rippon becomes the first woman ever to read the main evening news on BBC TV

1977

Women march to Reclaim the Night

Betty Williams and Mairead Corrigan who founded the Women's Peace Movement in Northern Ireland receive the Nobel Peace Prize

1978

Last Women's Liberation conference held

Black Women's group OWAAD formed

Louise Brown the world's 1st 'test tube' baby was born 26 July 1978

The Inland Revenue announced that all future correspondence and rebates will be sent directly to the wife and not the husband

1979

Margaret Thatcher becomes Britain's first woman PM

Southall Black Sisters formed

Portugal elects Maria Pintassilgo as the first female PM

Mother Teresa awarded the Nobel Peace Prize

Ayatollah Khomeini returns to Iran from exile and women see the return of the chador

1980

Vigdis Finnbogadottir elected as Iceland's first female president

Education Act frees Local Authorities from the provision of nursery care

Brighton Women's Football club win the European Cup for the last four years

50% of married women work outside of the home

100 protesters march through Brighton to protest against MP John Corrie's Abortion amendment bill, which aimed to tighten up the laws on abortion

1981

The House of Lords appoints Baroness Young as its first female leader

Gro Harlem Bruntland elected as Norway's first women PM

Susan Brown, the first woman cox, steers Oxford to victory in the boat race

One in four marriages ends in divorce

1982

Unemployment reaches three million between 1979 and 1986; women's unemployment rose by 276% compared to 146% for men

Government found guilty of failing to make provision for women to claim equal pay for work of equal value

Twenty thousand women join hands to encircle the Greenham Common airbase

1983

Mary Donaldson becomes the first woman Lord Mayor of London since the creation of the office in 1192

Removal of fair wages resolution hits low-paid women

1983 TUC announces guidelines on sexual harassment after pressure from the Women's Conference

November 1983 Janet Walton gives birth to six daughters after being treated with a fertility drug

1984

Following a ruling in the European courts the Government is forced to amend the equal pay act to allow women equal pay for work of equal value

50,000 women march through London to protest for striking miners

Brenda Dean is elected as the first woman to lead SOGAT 82 – a major trade union

1985

Child Benefit cut by 5%

The Law Lords reverse the ruling banning doctors from prescribing the pills to girls under 16

1986

Equal opportunities policies taken on by two hundred Local Authorities – NHS, Universities and police to follow

1986
Sexual harassment becomes illegal

Widow's Allowance scrapped

Qualifying age for women's pensions is raised

1987
Mrs Thatcher becomes the first Prime Minister to win a third successive term in office

41 women were elected to Parliament – 6% of the total membership of the House of Commons

Child Benefit frozen

1988
Child Benefit frozen for second year

Benazir Bhutto becomes the first woman ever elected to lead Pakistan

Section 28 bans schools and Local Authority-funded bodies from 'promoting homosexuality'

1989
Brighton Women's Centre moves to St. George's Mews

Women's average pay is still only 74% of men's average pay

80% of part-time workers are women

1990
Southall Black Sisters and Justice for Women take up cases of women imprisoned for murdering their violent husbands

The 1967 Abortion Act is amended and limits terminations from 28 weeks to 24

Thatcher resigns

A World Health Organisation report announces that AIDS is now the most common cause of death for women between the ages of 20 and 40

The Survivors Network for women survivors of child sexual abuse is founded in Brighton

1991
Helen Sharman became the first British woman in space

The Child Support Act is passed

House of Lords uphold decision that a husband can be charged with raping his wife

1992
CHAR – the housing campaign for single people, publish a report that four in ten of young women who become homeless have experienced sexual abuse

Kiranjit Ahluwalia sentenced to life for killing her violent husband is set free.

Women win the right to be ordained

1993
Abolition of Wages Council

Brighton Women's Centre hosts a national networking weekend for Women's Centres in the UK

1994
Arsonist causes £6,000 worth of damage at Brighton Women's Centre

1995

Transsexuals campaign to have official records altered

International Women's Conference in Beijing

Women of the Waterfront formed to support striking Liverpool Dockers

1996

Brighton Women's Centre gets first paid worker

In Afghanistan since the Taliban took power in 1996, women have had to wear burqua and have been beaten and stoned in public for not having the proper attire. Women are not allowed to work or even go out in public without a male relative. Professional women such as professors, translators, doctors, lawyers, artists and writers have been forced from their jobs.

1997

Princess Diana dies
Mother Teresa dies

1998

The average woman earns £15,438, the average man £21,877 – 30% more than the average woman

Aid worker Sally Becker from Brighton is shot in leg.

More than thirty-two thousand women diagnosed annually with breast cancer.

1999

Twenty-fifth anniversary of Brighton Women's Centre

Alanna

Alanna was born in Brighton and talks about her involvement in the Women's Centre and experiences of parenting and adopting her daughter.

I was involved in the Women's Centre in the early eighties and they had been donated a sum of money and we were trying to get them to buy a pool table. But they didn't do that. What they did instead was a few working-class women were picked to have a holiday abroad, of their choice, and I was one of them. They paid for me to go to Portugal for three weeks, plus expenses. At the time I was involved with a middle-class, white South African woman, so it was on the condition that she didn't go with me, even though we were living together. That was because I am a working-class woman, mixed-race, an incest survivor, so I was very 'right-on' and she didn't qualify. I was only allowed to have the money if she didn't go. Even if she paid with her own money, she wasn't allowed to come along. I stopped being involved [in the Women's Centre] because all the crap that was flying in terms of being in a certain category, if you were in a certain category, like me, I could do and say whatever I wanted, I could do no wrong. And in terms of my partner, who was none of those things… you know, just all the politics around all of that, I didn't want to be party to anymore, it was just quite horrific what was going on.

I worked as a volunteer on the Sussex Incest Crisis Line, with Sim. Sim set it up and wrote some article in *The Argus*, and I contacted her, so it was really just me and her that ran it. It was open about 4 times a week. Sim used to give talks at the Sussex Police HQ, at Social Services, we did an information leaflet. It closed down due to lack of funds. Because there were only two of us we couldn't do the fund raising as well. I got a lot out of it. Me being an incest survivor, it wasn't just me giving to the women, the women that I saw, I also ran a group twice a week, the women gave a hell of a lot back, in terms of mutual support. There was an older women's group and a younger women's group. They went on for about a year.

In 1990 my partner and I planned a child [through donor insemination] and it was decided that she had the baby, but it was also agreed at the time that she was having a baby for me, in terms of if we ever split up that the baby would stay with me. When my daughter was a few months old, we did go to a

Kate Downs
With immeasurable love.
From Alanna

Alanna

solicitor for me to adopt her. The solicitor advised us that because we were lesbians, that maybe we should wait until the child was about two or three, in terms of maybe the child being taken away from us. We had no problem with that.

When my daughter was two, my partner left me and that was quite frightening in terms of not just dealing with the pain of being left but also, the feelings of, I've got this child and all the decisions and everything is up to me now. I've got the main responsibility of bringing her up.

So that was like really hard. I'd wanted a child for so long that she was really really wanted. It was quite weird, why was I thinking this, I'm left alone with a child, whereas as a single person I would have still chosen to have a child. But it was maybe because I'd been involved with this person for a long time, and the plans we had made. Thinking, we're going to do this together. My ex-partner has got a commitment to my daughter, and she sees her once a week on a Saturday.

Last year, because I had no legal rights over my daughter and that was making me feel very insecure, I decided to go and see a solicitor and adopt her. I went to one solicitor first who actually was a lesbian and I chose her for that reason, and she said to me that my chances were really slim and that I probably wouldn't win the case. To get to foster her would be the best I could hope for. I just felt that, I'm not a foster parent, fostering for me is for a short period of time, and that child goes back to the mother, and that is not the case for me and my daughter. I would have actually got paid a weekly allowance until she reached sixteen. Also I would have been answerable on a lot of things to Social Services, and would have definitely had a social worker. So I found Donne, Mileham and Haddock, and they were brilliant. Right from the start they were brilliant, outlined that, yes, there were going to be a few problems and it wasn't going to be easy.

The Social Services had to assess me, assess my ex-partner, assess my daughter and her father, who's an old friend. My daughter sees him on a regular basis. They have a brilliant relationship, brilliant guy.

It was very difficult in terms of Social Services' questions. Issues like that my father is Anglo-Indian, and my daughter's father is Afro-Caribbean, and what kept on coming up was they have to place an Afro-Caribbean child with an Afro-Caribbean family. But she didn't need to be 'placed'– she had a family she had been with since birth. I kept on saying she is in close contact with her father and in terms of her culture, she will talk to him about that. And I'm not 100% white, and she goes to a very mixed race school, but that was a huge problem

Peggy Kathleen Majendie Brown
My mother – died in 1989 aged 72.
From Roz Cran

Alanna

for them. All they kept telling me was that I would have no problem fostering her, that I'd have 'x' amount of money a week, that I could have that until the child is 16, as if that was some kind of incentive. I was like, no, I'm not backing down here, and sometimes it was really hard, really stressful, and the questions that they would put at my daughter were really insensitive, saying to her that I wasn't her mum. Luckily she was told before that and because she has such a close relationship with her biological parent, there hasn't been a problem. She's discussed it with me, and also with her biological parent and her father. We've all been really open about this. I took her away for a weekend in London, we had a really nice weekend, and that's when I told her that I wanted to adopt her.

It took about a year to come to court and when we finally went there we wasn't in there five minutes. The judge was absolutely amazing and didn't even want to talk to Social Services. Just spoke to my daughter first and then spoke to me and that was it. It was a closed adoption. This means my ex-partner has no rights at all. I was going for an open adoption but for whatever reason the judge decided to grant a closed adoption. Which hasn't and will not effect my ex – in terms of what my daughter has with her biological parent is between them.

What makes our situation very different, is that I am not her biological mother. Yes I've adopted her but that was a first. That was a precedent. So she [my ex-partner] is biologically connected to this child, so maybe that's what keeps her connected to this child. Whereas it is usually the biological mother who stays put with the child, and the other one just walks away, and she feels maybe she can walk away because she's got no real connections with this child.

My daughter knows I'm a lesbian, and in lots of ways she does accept it. She says things like, do I love her dad, and I say yes, he's my friend, my close friend. Then she'll say why doesn't he live here with us. She does know quite a few children that are being brought up by lesbian mothers, and she accepts them. She remembers lots of things about when I was with her biological parent and she often likes to hear those stories, and also when I was involved since then with another woman she was totally fine about seeing two women together. That wasn't a problem. I think it's other things for her, her ideal would be that she lived with me and her father.

Betty Walshe

"Although it was Tory when I arrived, a year later Brighton went Labour. Then I moved from Brighton to Hove, which again, politically was a different kettle of fish, because Hove was then Tory. You may have gathered by now, I'm Labour, I have been all my life. I did set about giving Labour a higher profile in Hove and setting about raising the profile of women, because I think that that is very important in politics. Women have an awful lot to offer, there isn't enough of them in politics yet, although it's getting better. So I did set up a women's section and having done that, come '95, Labour took Hove, much to everybody's surprise, although not mine. And I became a Labour councillor in Hove.

A year later, the two towns of Brighton and Hove came together, and I was made Chair of the shadow Brighton and Hove Authority and then come the following year, 1997, I was made the first mayor of Brighton and Hove. I was particularly pleased about that because I thought it very fitting that the first Mayor of Brighton and Hove should be a woman.

Vixen Brown
My dearest wickedly funny, beautiful, non-judgmental friend.
From Kelle Kingsley

Betty Walshe

Being Mayor, of course, I was the Returning Officer, so I had the great honour of announcing the General Election results for all three constituencies, Brighton Pavilion, Kemp Town and Hove, and that was a wonderful experience. I read out Hove first and all my mates were down there crying their eyes out, everybody knew of course, we'd got in. I had to keep a straight face, I wasn't allowed to show any preference, and I thought, any minute, I'm going to start crying, but I got through that one and then of course back to Brighton and by now it was two or three in the morning and they were cheering, they just wouldn't shut up you see, and in the end I had to shout 'Do you want to hear the results or not', so then they did shut up, just long enough for me to read out the results and by then I too was cheering with them.

It was all so fantastic, and needless to say I didn't get to bed that night because after that there was much celebration. So yes, it was wonderful, and I'm jolly glad…It's been my one wish that I should live long enough to see another Labour government. But of course, now that I've seen it, I want it to keep going for a pretty long time anyway.

I am a Socialist and I think it started because when I was young, in my teens, I thought well, there's something wrong here, things have got to be better, mainly because of my childhood and everything seemed so one-sided, with few people well off and then the poverty and hardship, and it just didn't seem to be fair. I thought, there must be something better, so then I started looking into it and reading up and it was funny really because my husband already was a Socialist. We hadn't up until then discussed politics in the home and he came home one day – I was quite young, still in my early 20s – and he said 'I've enrolled us both in the Labour Party' and not being one to be pushed around, I said 'what do you mean, what is this Labour Party?', 'it's the political party, the one that we should belong to, it's Socialism' so I said ' you have no right to enrol me in anything without me being consulted' so I went storming over to the secretary who runs the Labour Party where I lived then – Chelmsford – which wasn't really much hope for Labour then, never mind, and so I said, 'what is this?' and I then sat down with them and discussed it all and then when he'd finished I said 'yes, that's for me' and that was 45 years ago and I've been a member ever since.

My childhood started off all right, and it would have been all right. My mother was, for the want of a better word, middle class, but unfortunately my father died when I was 18 months old and I already had a sister, she was 7 and my

Betty Walshe

brother wasn't born. In 1929, there was nothing to support women on their own and my mother didn't even get a widow's pension, it would only have been ten bob, but she didn't even get a widow's pension, simply because my father had not paid into it. So of course we had nothing. She had to sell up all that she had, her home, in order to pay the funeral bills. Obviously I can imagine that there was mad panic. It must have been pretty dreadful.

My aunt took me in and my brother, who was born six months after my father's death, went to foster parents, and my sister – there was obviously much searching around – was sent to what was then called an orphanage – it was actually an asylum for fatherless children. It was opened in 1840, I don't think that it had changed much since then. I went when I was three, my brother went when he was two. I shall never forget my first day, my mother said I was going to school and of course I was so proud that I was going to school, I'd been bought a new coat. I remember walking up a very long drive, it was a huge building, it held 300 children from the age of 18 months until the leaving age, which was then 15. It had everything, its own church, own hospital, school, everything.

Walking up this drive I saw this great huge building, I was this little tiny thing of three years old. I remember going into this room. Obviously I was taken into, for the want of a better word, what was called a nursery, and there was a rocking horse, my mother, because she was trying to… she must have been pretty nervous herself, she said 'look at that lovely rocking horse'. I go over to it, to please her and I turn around and she was gone. And that was it.

I was there ten years, it was pretty awful. Although we were two sisters and a brother, we never saw each other because my brother came after I had gone up to the infants; he was with the babies, then I went into the girls'. By then my sister was 13 and so of course she was one of the big girls and they didn't associate with the little girls. And my brother went to the boys' side and I never saw him. I used to worry about my brother, because the time when boys and girls sat together – in the same room, although, at different sides – was when we ate, and that was long tables with forms, we weren't allowed to speak, and if you spoke, you either had to stand on the form for the rest of the meal, you didn't have any more to eat, or you left the room. You weren't meant to leave anything, but the food was so appaling that more often than not we did, and there were rat holes, so we put it down the rat holes. I think that we must have had the best fed rats

Betty Walshe

in the country. We would watch the rats at night. There were long dormitories with about 30 beds in each and at night we would watch the rats playing on the roof. In the winter it was bitterly cold, we weren't very well fed, the clothes were inadequate and the discipline was very, very harsh. There was no love. I missed my mother terribly for the whole of the ten years that I was there. I pined for my mother.

Now we come to the war. My education really ceased at twelve because that's when we spent most of the time down the shelters, because the school was very near London. Then at thirteen my sister had already left and she – because she was obviously not happy at home, joined the Women's Army – the ATS – much against my mother's will. My mother wrote some sort of pitiful letter to the school and asked if I could leave. You weren't really allowed to because when the mothers left their children at the school, they signed a contract, they signed their children away, that they would not take their children away until the age of 15 unless they married. These were the only two ways you could leave Reedham. The headmaster – which was very unwise of him I think – called me in and asked me did I want to leave? Well, seeing as I had dreamt of nothing else for ten years, of course I said yes, but it was a mistake, because having reached home, this wonderful woman I had dreamed of, wasn't the woman I had expected, so my idol fell and I was broken hearted. And then, believe it or not, I cried every night for a year to go back. I then had five not very happy years at home.

We lived in East Grinstead then, this was where the burns unit was and that was full of burnt airmen and so I met my husband. He was a badly burnt airman, and I wasn't in very good shape myself so we were a right pair. I married at 18 and we moved to Chelmsford and that was all quite eventful, because I knew nothing about life. However, we weathered it through and then in 1949 our first son was born, but then we had got a council flat, the housing situation was as bad then as it is today, which I find appaling. We were allotted a prefab, an aluminium bungalow, they were only meant to stand twenty years, they are still standing.

It was there that our second, third and fourth sons were born – all boys. When the eldest was 12 we moved to Crawley. I do have to say – although I don't want to dwell on it too much – my marriage wasn't particularly happy and so we did feel that if we moved back to Sussex – because I did miss Sussex – I also felt it would be a good thing for my husband to get nearer the hospital. He managed to get a job, two sons went to university, and I opened a play group and after three years I sold that and

Betty Walshe

went into industry. I worked my way up, by then I was quite active in the Labour Party too, and I became a Shop Steward in the union there and I did improve the working conditions and the wages of the women in the factory, which were quite appaling. I had twelve happy years in industry and meanwhile three sons had got to university, one had graduated, had a child, the second one had married. Then my husband was taken ill with lung cancer and I therefore packed up work and looked after him. He was told he had six months to live, he lived for five months.

I married very young. My husband was eight years older than me, so therefore I was his little girl and I knew nothing of the world anyway and this situation did continue until, and it's quite funny really, well first of all, I was in my 20's and I did pick up the Betty Friedan book, *The Feminine Mystique*, she was really the first feminist writer. I read that and I thought, well there's something wrong with my life here and then when my eldest son was 14, I was doing his room when I found under his bed *The Second Sex* by Simone De Beauvoir, I sat downstairs and didn't get up until I'd finished it. When he came home I said 'I've found this book under your bed, but I think you are possibly a bit too young for it' and he said 'well to tell you the truth mum I don't understand it'. However I gave it back to him for when he was older.

That was really the best thing that happened to me and after that I wanted to know more. So then I ordered from the library *The Female Eunuch*, and there was me in my thirties, with four children and the librarian – a man – said when I ordered it 'do you realise what this is about?' and I said 'of course I do, what do you think I'm ordering it for?' So I read that, so you could say then that Germaine Greer did change my whole life, my whole outlook on life and my behaviour and everything about my life because then I started to stick up for myself, to speak for myself so my marriage did break, that really did do it, because of course his 'little girl' disappeared completely.

So then I was a campaigner for women's rights and I brought my boys up as the nearest thing that you can get to feminism in a man and now as men, I think that, dare I say, I am quite proud of them, because I do have to admit I don't really think too much of the male sex, but my sons have turned out pretty good. There is no such thing in their households as men's and women's work, or men's place and women's place and I think their partners would walk out if there was and quite rightly so.

Sharon Doherty
A friendship still strong after fifteen years! Here's hoping we both find what we're looking for by the next fifteen!
From Jane Wilkin

Betty Walshe

So I'm still fighting for women, it still is a struggle, we still haven't yet got there and this is what I hope young women realise. I hope that they don't think that this is how it is and this is how it's going to be because it won't unless they fight for it. The fight isn't over and if young women sit back they will lose all that we have achieved. They will lose the struggle, because men still want it all, you have only got to look at all the men leaders, all the men in power.

As a councillor on a huge estate where there is a lot of poverty and single parents, and if you are a woman and a single parent, life is harder. Most women – if they are able to work – their salary is much lower, and if you are looking after a small child it's very difficult to work, children are people, they are not machines. And so usually there is very little money in the home and I have found it terribly distressing, some of the women who I go to see want help and I have felt so helpless, because there is so little you can do. I am not a stranger to poverty and I'm not a stranger to suffering but even when I see it in other people, I find it very distressing.

I am still a member of CND, I marched in all the marches in London. When Greenham Common was set up – and don't forget all this time I was battling at home, everything that I took part in I had to fight for at home and it wasn't easy, whether it was to go to Labour Party meetings, or to go on a march. At the peace marches, my youngest son did join me, which was good, so then Greenham Common was set up and I went up like thousands of women, I went up to all the big national days and then after my husband had died I went on night watches, then you went up for a night and you took over from the women so that they could have a night off. However, that was very difficult for them as I regret to say that the army and the police made noises all night to keep them up.

And then there was the miners' strike. I used to sit outside the Co-Op in Kemp Town collecting parcels and then I went down to a mining town in Dorset. We stayed the night in a miner's home and we went along to the miners' club attached to the mine. The Tories have now closed that, it's gone. I was in the mining club and what do we get onto? – women. And as much as one must support the miners, they are your typical male, so they were saying 'with equality women can go down the mines now if they want'. Nobody has the right to say that a woman can't do anything. If a woman wants to do something then she is entitled to do it, just the same for men, if a man wants to be a mid-wife or a

Betty Walshe

nurse, then good luck to him. This miner was saying 'oh women shouldn't be allowed down the mines' and of course we were having a good old humdinger, so even though I was supporting them, in the end I was falling out with them, and I don't suppose for one minute that I got him to see my point of view, which is that no one has any right to deny a woman any aspect of life that she wants to do.

To the young women of Brighton I say, don't give up, don't go to sleep – the fight isn't over – stick with it. Brighton is a great place to live and Brighton people are wonderful and from the day I arrived I was never a stranger, it is the Brighton people that make Brighton the great place that it is.

To all the wild women of Brighton...
From Melita Dennett

Deirdre and Elizabeth Counihan

Deirdre has lived in Brighton for much of her life, while Elizabeth has only just recently moved back to Brighton after more than 20 years.

Deirdre: We were brought up in Brighton when we were little because my mum lived in Brighton during the war. In fact in the streets around here [the Port Hall area] she can remember when this was fields and she can remember going to the farm to get eggs and things just down the road. A lot of these houses around here have been built since she was around.

We were sent to the Sacred Heart Convent, which is now Cardinal Newman, and then we moved to College Terrace, Kemp Town and we went to what was then the Blessed Sacrament Convent, now the Junior School of Brighton College, so I'm teaching in the old dormitory of where Liz and I were at school which is really very weird. And then after that we moved up to London for quite a bit. I think they lost a lot of money over the house in College Terrace, it was a very big house.

Elizabeth: And then they moved back to Sussex but not to Brighton, we lived near East Grinstead for quite a long time.

Deirdre: One of our brothers died and we wanted to move after that, so we moved back to Brighton. I was at the Art College at that time and Elizabeth was at medical school, but I used to walk round Brighton and I saw this big tall house in Powis Square and I thought 'that would just suit us', so I more or less persuaded my parents to move to Brighton, because I didn't want to have to come to college on the train. I more or less twisted their arms and we moved into this big house in Powis Square, which was amazing, lived in by one little old lady, it had been flats and it was all front doors all the way up when we moved in. We were a very big family – there were seven of us, so we all had our own rooms for the first time.

Elizabeth: I didn't live there really, I was at medical school.

Deirdre: I was there all the time, I was at Brighton Art College, I did my teacher training after Brighton Art College. Then I got married to my first husband and he taught at De La Salle School, which was what the Sacred Heart Convent turned into. Then he got a job in Oxford so we moved, and then we moved to Glasgow and then to Henley and then we finally got back to Brighton just as my marriage broke up. I ended up in Brighton with two little boys for a long time, and our other sister was on her own with one child. We all came back. It was very nice coming back to Brighton because it was a place where you could be a single mum quite easily, I mean you can live cheaply in Brighton. I managed to live off Social Security and I didn't get into debt, and I'm really quite proud that I managed to do that because I wasn't being lent any money or anything, I really was living off it, not for very long.

Then I got a job, first of all at that funny little Windlesham School, along Dyke Road. It was all single mums on their own, you were made to work terribly long hours, I really got quite ill doing that and then my younger one Mark got ill and I had to stop, to be at home looking after him. I was living in Coventry Street then, I tried going back to doing art work and things and I was sitting doing little rows of mice for a potter, all these little mice, to sort of try and earn a crust. And then Mark got a bit better and they both went to Cottesmore, both the boys and then I got a job at Davies's and I got Head of Art, in graphic design and everything, which what I was properly qualified to do.

That was a very good job and things were sort of all right after that and then my first husband died which again, well, you know we'd divorced, but he died and that really was absolutely awful and I couldn't afford to go paying the

Deirdre and Elizabeth Counihan

Mary Minetta White
for always being there with an endless supply of strength and unconditional love. Thank you.
From Lisa J Saidi

Deirdre and Elizabeth Counihan

mortgage any more and then I went to live in a house with Nick who was a family friend, then we finally got married and we came here when we got married. So we were in Coventry Street, then Lancaster Road for a bit and then we moved in here and we've been here ever since. I was on my own with the kids for six years and I did quite a lot of freelance art.

Elizabeth: The medical school that I went to did have probably about 30% women, whether it was actually restricted I don't know. The Royal Free had more, the Royal Free was almost entirely women, at that time. There were fewer medical schools that's the other thing, there just weren't the places anyway.

I always wanted to move back to Brighton again, I didn't really particularly like living in East Grinstead – it's rather dull. So when I chucked up the full time job I decided to come back to Brighton just as soon as I could manage. You know, I had to sort of be able to afford it so I had to save up quite a lot of money and sell my other house and so on, because I didn't want to work full time any more. So I chucked up my full time job three years ago and moved down here six months ago. My kids are like hers, they're grown up now, they're both off my hands now. I don't have to pay for anyone's education any more.

Deirdre: It was very hard for her to be a doctor, I mean I always felt that.

Elizabeth: It wasn't any harder for me than anyone else.

Deirdre: I don't know, I always felt that women had to be a little better actually somehow to succeed.

Elizabeth: Yes, I suppose that's probably true. Yes, probably getting into medicine you had to be that much better, but I mean I don't think it was anything terrific you know. I wanted to be a GP, I didn't want to be a consultant. I think if you want to be a consultant then you probably would come up against more problems. But it is true that when I first went in to General Practice I was the only woman doctor in the area at all. I'd taken over from another woman, but I was the only one in the area. Now of course everyone has a woman doctor, patients rather like them actually. Women doctors get far more work than the men because they just like women doctors much more.

Deirdre: It's the attitude towards earning, which you probably haven't felt as much as me because you know doctors earn pretty good money.

Elizabeth: Women and men doctors don't earn any different.

Deirdre and Elizabeth Counihan

Deirdre: Of course women and men teachers don't earn any different – unless you're at a private school – but I must say I noticed it very much in the attitude of my first husband, that when I ceased to earn because I had the two small children, my value went right down and I remember his mother who was in fact a very liberated woman in the 1920s, I mean she did the most astonishing things, I remember her talking to me about it being 'his money' and I could nearly have hit her. I find my present husband, who's a lot younger than me, his attitude to women's earnings and everything is quite different. Just in my own age group the men had a very, very poor attitude they expected the women to do all the things in the house and look after the children, but they expected them to earn as well.

Elizabeth: My ex-husband was a bit like that, he's the same sort of age as me and his attitude was certainly that if he helped out in the house it was because he was being kind. It wasn't like his job.

Deirdre: 'Look I'm doing it for you darling'… It's true that these days, there is little to remark on in a woman being a doctor or a teacher (I am rather ashamed of working as a teacher in fact – maybe I should have been more single-minded about my art career). It is perfectly normal to be bringing up kids on one's own, nor is it news that some men are stupid and selfish.

What we do think we have achieved, and are proud of, is that, as well as being single mothers and doing full-time jobs, we have earned recognition in an unexpected and very male-dominated field, i.e. the production of *Scheherazade* – a successful Science Fiction magazine – which we run on what amounts to feminist principles of respect for authors and artists.

Science Fiction and Fantasy are very important aspects of modern writing. Where do you think the roots of the ecology movement were, if not in S.F.? Where do you think such issues as global warming were first discussed?

I would go so far as to say that the S.F. genre can represent the cutting edge of literature. The fact that it can also be terrific fun and sells like hot cakes shouldn't detract from its intrinsic value – having fun is valuable in itself, after all. Liz and I feel that it's essential that the woman's viewpoint should be voiced within this medium.

It so happens that Brighton is a notable focus of S.F. writing, which is one of the reasons that we are so glad to live here.

For my family and friends (you know who you are) who have always loved, supported and encouraged me –
Thank you.
From Tanya Levene

Debbie Harris

Debs owns her own company which she runs from home. She lives in Hove with her husband and two children, Luke and Maddy – at the time of this interview Maddy was 13 weeks old.

"I was born in Dorset, I was an illegitimate child. Mum met my adopted Dad and we went to Italy, then Brazil, then we ended up in Horsham. Then Mum decided that she didn't want to do travelling anymore and she wanted a settled environment so we moved to Partridge Green, where we had some land and horses, so it was a lovely childhood. I got a sales assistant job at Branch which is in Brighton, met Tim and just stayed around here ever since.

I started work after leaving college, and I started as just a sales assistant in an engineering firm. I had no idea what I was going to do and my mother was a nurse so I decided 'well I'll be a nurse', I got accepted for the London School of Nursing but they couldn't take me for six months. So I decided to do a local business course. My mother left my father, I had two younger sisters and I had to stay and look after them. I developed an aptitude for engineering and just went higher

Debbie Harris

and higher and higher, and eventually became the sales manager. I realised earlier on that if I wanted a family and children there was no way I could do it in that environment. I was very, very ambitious and when I was talking to the guy that owned the whole thing – a directorship was on the cards for me, but it was very clearly, craftily asked if I was going to have children? And of course I said 'no' – like you do, when you're that age, you don't think you'll have children anyway, but in the back of my mind was, well if I don't have children, life's not going to really fulfil itself. At the time I can remember feeling really cross and angry about it but not knowing what I could really do about it.

I met my current husband in 1985, we had a one-bedroomed flat, a really nice lifestyle, he had a good job, I had a good job, but at the end of the month, no money and we decided that the only way we could actually have children or family life was not to live off two salaries. We had a go at putting one salary aside but that didn't work and then I just got all hormonal and jacked in my job and decided right that's it, I'm just going to have to do something else, working for myself or something.

There's no way you can easily have a family and a full-time job. I did desk-top publishing and things like that for people, because my great hobby was computers. Then I got pregnant with Luke and then we decided to get married and then we were really, really broke, incredibly broke, you couldn't get any help from the DSS as my husband's salary was just above the limit. I looked into it and decided that the only way we could get out of the rut without me going back to full-time work was to actually rent out my flat and buy a house in my husband's name, and that's what I did. We moved into my mother-in-law's for three hellish months, whilst the house purchase was going through. We got there and then at least we had the two bedrooms and so I started a telephone marketing business with a partner in the second bedroom.

We've now got 9 people that we employ. We won an award quite a while ago for women in business, which was a real boost.

When you have a young child you do actually need to be able to get out and talk to other people in the same situation. Now, I found with Luke, a lot of women were very much at home and totally resigned to being at home. If there was a Centre where I could go to where there were people in a very similar situation to me, that would be brilliant, but it's just finding a place like that. I don't really know what the Brighton Women's Centre's all about, apart from giving you information, if you're in a 'desperate state' – which I'm not in.

Nikki Avery
for being such a fantastic person.
From Emma Seers

Debbie Harris

There's no such thing as equality, I don't think. What is equality? Being treated equal – but you're never going to be, there's females and there's males and they are different. The women have the time of the month, they have the menopause, they have the children. They have this awful thing that you cannot leave your child. I've had rows with my husband where he's said 'sod you then' and just gone out, and I could do that and it's packing up two children, the nappies and stuff and getting in the car – where do I go? Even something as basic as that means that you can never have that true equality.

We're bringing up Luke to help and be part of the family as an equal male, that he does his fair share. He clears the table, empties the dishwasher that sort of thing. But Tim's mother didn't really expect Tim to do much, she still irons his shirts because I refuse to. I think it's a generation thing. I'm too busy and I'm not doing that, it's been a long upward struggle in order to get my husband to do his share. If you're a mother and you're at home, you're termed as 'you don't work'.

A man can get so involved with children but they can't actually do all the things we do. We have the monthly cycle, pregnancy and childbirth, breast feeding and letting go of your child, it's all such strong emotions and you feel really alive all the time. I don't think that a man could actually get that.

When Maddy was born, I got the baby blues and I got very, very upset because I looked at her and I thought, right she's either going to have a child and go through that childbirth which is pretty horrendous. Or if she doesn't actually want to have children, when she looks out and sees that it's just not kind to bring a child into the world, or she might not be able to conceive a child which must be the most awful anguish ever. When I was younger, at college, I really didn't want children, then the hormones just changed and if you don't have that I feel you must miss out on a whole bunch of life.

Erica Mackenzie

Erica came to Brighton from London after two years of more or less full-time unemployment and depression to rebuild her life and start again.

I'd had to sell my flat and get rid of a lot of my property. I felt that all I was went with it. And the future? Well, I couldn't see one. But I had to make one. But where?

Brighton! Well, I'm a dyke! So I came to Brighton. The only good thing about the DSS was that the disability employment officer sent me down to the Women's Centre. A place which I would never have dared go to if I hadn't been sent. This wasn't because I didn't know that Women's Centres existed, but I sound like and look like a middle-class woman. Actually my origins are dead ordinary and dead poor and dead difficult and disturbed. But I went to university, so I was educated out of my background into a no-man's land in class terms. And I knew that Women's Centres didn't think of themselves as being for women like me, nor did I think of them being for women like me.

So had it not been for the disability employment officer sending me there, wild horses wouldn't have dragged me there. Now, a year later, I still have a connection and it's been useful. It's led to my getting a maths 'O' Level. I'm building a new life, and I guess it's all beginning to come together now but it's been a painful business getting here.

One of the things about the modern economic structure is that there is structural unemployment and it affects all age groups. It affects people who are just coming out of university, or school and they can't get jobs. Those in their late twenties, and in their thirties, people who have never had more than six months' shit work, as well as affecting middle-aged people. It's not something that just affects my age group, it's structural, it's the way things are all across Europe, that relatively few people have work and they are being worked to death, and the rest have nothing, or not enough. It's a terrible political problem which isn't being addressed.

In a place like Brighton there's a far greater tolerance and solidarity between people in different circumstances. I think cities are merciless actually. Why did my blood have to run cold and life become so thin before I realised how inhumane London was?

Sexism and the position of women rears its ugly head at every opportunity. Some things have changed but not enough. I honestly don't think that anything will seriously change until men are socialised differently. And women are partly responsible for the way men are socialised. No, I think certain latitude is now given to

Lorraine Whitby for being my oldest friend and being so supportive and there for me when we were kids.
From Emma Seers

Erica Mackenzie

women in certain quarters, but there are glass ceilings, women still occupy most low-paid, part-time jobs with no security, and have all the main responsibility for child rearing and child care.

I've always been an 'out' lesbian, and that has not been easy. So my politics is with a small 'p' in my life, I'm not interested in ideology or political dogma for itself. I'm interested in its affect on people, in social justice. I really don't want to talk much about the position of women and how much it's changed, except that I'd have hoped it would have changed more and I feel rather despairing that it hasn't.

We have a working world which demands that if women are to succeed at all they have got to work twice as hard as any man. On top of that they've got to work impossible inhumane hours, to prove their commitment, and that they are as good as the next man, who believes he is better than everybody else put together for no good reason. And on top of that, they have got almost total domestic responsibility and I think it's just impossible. And women are crucifying themselves thinking that it is possible. It's the same as it ever was.

The most significant event in my life was the death, 20 years ago, of somebody whom I loved very much and who loved me more than anybody had ever loved me before or since. And against which the calamities which have brought me to Brighton, are as nothing. I'm crying now as I say it, but actually the most wonderful thing about that, the most character forming thing is, that I wouldn't be who I am now if it hadn't been for that. If I hadn't been loved like that, and lost it, I wouldn't be who I am now. I wouldn't be me. Her name was Karin. She was my best friend. We loved each other with a passion. For nearly seven years of my life, from 19 to 26. I had always expected to grow old with her. She was killed in an air crash. She wasn't even 30.

The grieving took years. You can't authenticate the grief all the time. It took years. It took about seven years before I removed a gold chain from around my neck which she had given me. The only time I removed it was when I thought it would be in danger. But it was like a part of me which I couldn't bear to be without. After seven years I found myself taking it off very easily one day, and I knew that was a very significant moment. Now, Karin is part of who I am.

I'm nearly 47 now, and I guess when I'm 80 I'll be saying it with the same feeling. She is very present to me, in my everydayness. In the times when I'm in trouble, so she's part of who I am. I knew when she died that I'd be lucky if I ever had a love like that again. And I haven't.

Karin's life and death has had the most terrific impact on my life. All of it.

Karin Monath
born Dasswil, near Bonn, West Germany, 15 April 1948. Died 18 December 1977 off the island of Madeira. Taken care of by the vast Atlantic. Still my beloved friend after all these years.
From Erica Mackenzie

Erica Smith

Erica came to Brighton in 1986 after graduating from a graphic design course in Reading.

"I remember Brighton from when I was a little kid, because we always had our holidays in the Ashdown Forest, about 25 miles to the North. I remember coming down here with my mum and she'd rummage through these horrible little second-hand shops looking at old forks and spoons and stuff and I'd get really bored and embarrassed by her hunting for old tat. I never thought I'd move to Brighton and do exactly the same thing – scavenging through the North Laine and boot sales and charity shops. I think Brighton is a great town – I know a lot of people who move here because if you have to live in the UK, this is the best place to live.

I first went to Brighton Women's Centre quite soon after I moved here – although I can't remember how I found out about it. I wanted to find a sympathetic doctor, and I knew they kept a directory of women doctors. The Centre was in a basement up from the Old Steine at the time. I think I must have disturbed a committee meeting when I knocked on the door, but I told

Helen Aekers
who was a lovely friend, stalwart supporter and who gave me a home when I needed it. She is sorely missed.
From Dee Bridgewood

Erica Smith

someone what I wanted, and I sat and read through the directory whilst the other women carried on with their discussion.

When I first moved here I only knew two people – a friend from school and a girl I knew from college. It actually took me quite a long time to meet people that I really had a lot in common with, and I felt quite lonely at first. I'd say it took me about two years before I felt really settled here and felt at home. One of the ways I got to know more people was going back to the Women's Centre (which was now in Lettice House) and getting involved in producing the very first issues of *Broadsheet*.

At that time I'd just set up as a self-employed graphic designer on the Enterprise Allowance Scheme, and as I got busier with that I got less involved with Broadsheet, but I enjoyed being part of the newsletter team. It was a great opportunity to meet some really nice women, and it was quite an eye-opening experience too! I'm proud of being in at the beginning of Broadsheet, and I have always enjoyed reading the latest issue whenever it comes out.

I've always been a feminist, and have always had feminist friends, and valued the support of my female friends and housemates. But, apart from that short period with Broadsheet, I've never been directly involved in women's groups or something like the Women's Centre. I'm not really much of a 'joiner', and tend to remain a bit aloof – not really an 'activist', but somewhere bobbing around on the scene. If something annoys me I'm more likely to go out and take direct action as an individual – graffiti on a sexist poster, for example.

I think that's partly why I decided to start *GirlFrenzy* as well – because there were things that I wanted to comment on that I felt weren't really covered anywhere else. I thought I'd create my own forum for debate and discussion – and also publicise the work of women comic artists because they weren't getting any coverage anywhere else!

I was walking down Lansdowne Place to the 7-11 sometime in 1990 and the name 'GirlFrenzy' popped into my head. I thought it would be a great name for a band, but then I thought no, I can't sing or play guitar – if I was in a band I'd do two gigs and they'd be awful and that would be a waste of the name. I'd recently been reading comics again, and I'd been amazed at how few comics portrayed women in a sensitive way, and very, very few comics, if any, that you could buy commercially were written or drawn by women. I decided that GirlFrenzy would be a good name for a magazine which covered issues such as women comic artists which were not given coverage anywhere else.

Irene
To a loving grandmother.
From Tom

Erica Smith

I'd also just discovered Valerie Solanas – I think *The SCUM Manifesto* is a very interesting publication and I was really surprised at how low a profile it had at this time. I wanted to produce a magazine which would feature something like the SCUM Manifesto – but not in a way that would immediately be categorised as 'serious feminism' – like *Spare Rib* – and only be read by a converted audience.

I really like the idea of having a balance between comic art and alternative feminist theories, so there is a double audience. Because of its comic input, as many men as women read GirlFrenzy, and they therefore end up reading articles from a women's point of view which they might otherwise be oblivious to. At the same time I wanted to promote the work of comic artists to people who generally don't read comics – and on the whole, women are much less likely to read comics than men.

I was putting together the first GirlFrenzy at the time of Poll Tax. I was working, and had the money to pay Poll Tax, but I didn't approve of it – it was so clearly an unfair tax on the poor. I decided I'd keep my Poll Tax money in a separate account and save it up until I had enough to pay for printing the first issue of GirlFrenzy – and that's just what I did!

I had a fantasy that the bailiffs would come round and demand money or goods to the value of my unpaid Community Charge. Then I could hand them boxes of GirlFrenzy and say: 'The cover price is 90p, here's 1,000 – go out and sell them. You can keep the change!'. The reality is that GirlFrenzy sold out really quickly without any attempt at publicity or promotion. It just got picked up by the music press and given rave reviews, and people went out and bought copies.

I got people to contribute to GirlFrenzy by handing out flyers at the Small Press Fair in London, and I asked friends to do something for me, and wrote to women comic artists in the States. Because the USA is such a big country, and more comic-friendly, there are more women comic artists there – and some even make a living from the comics industry. Some really well-known comic artists like Trina Robbins and Mary Fleener wrote back to me with comic strips and articles. Trina Robbins wrote a really interesting article for the first issue about Sex and Sexism in comics. So right from the first issue I had a good range of stuff to publish – from women who had never drawn a comic strip before to women with a high profile.

The flyer said something like 'not Cosmo, not Spare Rib but GirlFrenzy' and described it as a publication 'By women for women'. That annoyed some women as well as men. Even now I get men asking if they can contribute, and I say yes, you can, but you have to cut your dick off first – that shuts them up!

Joan Counihan
(nee Newton) born in 1915, brought up a family of seven children just after the war (difficult times – no servants and yet no gadgets) and went on to become an historian and expert on the life and work of Victorian pioneer antiquarian Mrs Ella Armitage.
From Deirdre and Elizabeth Counihan

Erica Smith

There are plenty of other places where men can get their comics and articles published. Until there is a 50/50 balance of men and women in the media at large, GirlFrenzy will remain an all female publication.

Right from the start, some of the articles in GirlFrenzy have caused offence to some people. Trina Robbins' article about sex and sexism in comics included some explicit illustrations by male artists such as Robert Crumb, but I felt it was fair to include them in the context of a discussion about sexism. Another article which some people found tasteless was an interview with a woman which raised the issue of paedophilia. From the age of 13 she had been sexually active with older men, and by 15, with older women – within relationships she felt were not exploitative or abusive since she had chosen to enter those relationships as an equal partner. Everybody has to work out for themselves at what age they become a sexually active person – and whether new sexual practices are disgusting and exploitative or just another part of their life.

I know this is a touchy subject and I don't cover such issues to be voyeuristic or exhibitionistic – I think GirlFrenzy is a safe arena for them to be raised. People have desires which they express in different ways – and those desires might not be 'politically correct'. I don't think there is anything intrinsically wrong with drawing or writing or sharing fantasies – but putting them into practice can be a different matter. There is a darker side to everyone, and I think it is better to discuss such things rather than hide them away and pretend they don't exist.

I'm not sure if there is the same need for GirlFrenzy as there was in 1991 when the first issue came out. Valerie Solanas and anti-censorship feminists and fat liberation have all been widely covered in recent years. But it's not fair to say there is no need for feminism anymore – that this is a post-feminist society. You only have to look at the number of men at the top, and the fact that women are still earning significantly less than men. And if they are earning as much or more money, they are actually doing at least two jobs – because they are still doing all the domestic work at home. I find it deeply disturbing that even within my circle of 'enlightened' friends, women are still doing nearly all the bloody housework as well as going out and earning more money than their male partners.

I think we're at an interesting time in society, because women are beginning to take a more active role – but at great sacrifices to themselves. And I think men have got a lot of catching up to do – as women move in to the traditionally male role of breadwinner, organiser, decision-maker, men also need to get used to performing traditional female roles like housework,

Erica Smith

emotional care and childcare. I think it will take a long time for men to adapt and there will be a real struggle over the next few years. Already the trend is being set that young women are getting jobs whilst young men don't seem to have comparable social or domestic skills. And if people are going to carry on having kids, there has to be equality within parenting and the domestic sphere. That is not happening at the moment.

I'd like to think that Brighton will be at the forefront of these kind of social changes. It IS a different world compared to the rest of the UK. I grew up in the north west, and it is true that people are friendlier up north – but only if you fit in with everyone else. Brighton isn't as friendly, but it is a lot more tolerant. Despite its *Brighton Rock* razor-gang history, I think it is a real soft place to live. I never feel threatened walking home on my own at night. The fact that Brighton is 'right-on', that it has a huge gay community and lots of artists and academics and weirdos means that it appeals to people like me who move here for that atmosphere. I find it really funny that walking past a building site in Brighton, if I'm going to get a cat-call it will be 'nice boots!' rather than a comment about my anatomy. Only in Brighton would you get such fashion-conscious builders!

Helen Elliot
– for finding her courage.
From Vicki Brown

Helen Zahavi

A woman of dangerous imagination, Zahavi had an overwhelming 180º revolution of consciousness in Brighton in the long hot summer of 1988. She changed from a woman who felt vulnerable, threatened, too scared to walk along the beach at night, to a writer of slasher revenge. She is the author of best-seller, *Dirty Weekend* and *True Romance*.

I lived in Brunswick Place, Hove and there were fights outside my window. I saw one bloke beat up his girlfriend. I saw two blokes with two-foot staves. I got paranoid, then the physical fear fed through to rage and that feeling became Bella (the central character in *Dirty Weekend*). In 1988, a series of attacks on women in Brunswick town led the police to recommend that single women stayed indoors with their windows shut – not very pleasant in a heat wave. At the back, my flat was overlooked by thirty other windows. Someone was watching me and I had threatening calls. One night I went and stared at those windows and felt such overwhelming rage that I was scared of them and they were not scared of me. I had always seen myself as a victim. The thought of climbing out of my flat and crossing over to those other windows was liberating. I was a liberal *Guardian* reader having exciting murderous fantasies. Not quite erotic, but nearly! I began to imagine doing it, I began to write it down, and that became the character. Just me and my computer. I was not imagining anyone else – it was my story.

I hate confrontation and arguments. I was repressed most of my life and when I let go it came with force. Bella became my id. She went around slaying my monsters. When the police told us 'don't sleep with your windows open', I became furious that you have to live like a prisoner, a mole, a convict. I realised I'm trapped by my psychology. There's a blurring between the nice feminine female and it's a differential politics. I was nasty, aggressive and unable to express my aggression. My life was stunted by fear of attack and causing offence. There was a rage of recognition when I realised I didn't have a raised consciousness. I came to the moment – it was a combination of factors – the phone calls, seeing people beaten up, feeling trapped and a lot of self-loathing.

Some women were enraged by my depiction of female fear and vengeance. Mostly a certain type of middle-class female journalist. They refused to acknowledge that a woman has a

Helen Zahavi

right to defend herself – there's a right to use violence to defend a child, but it's unwomanly to defend yourself. Men identified with Bella the underdog fighting back. You have a right in law to defend yourself. But some of the reviews were hysterical. It became clear I was hitting a nerve.

Brighton, with its piers and edgy atmosphere, is a unique town. There's nowhere like it. It's always inspired filmmakers and writers. I'm always thinking of moving back. There are social problems – poverty, a great deal of homelessness. People feeling frustrated and angry can express themselves certain ways. There's a slow burning social fuse. It's very dynamic, with all these different people thrown together. Then there's the social side, and the London-by-sea side, and the art/crime side.

When I'm writing it comes out in an organic way, it's not schematic. I love Bella, I don't like this one [the heroine in *True Romance*]. She's interesting and I'd like to have her round for dinner but not to stay the night. [*True Romance*] was inspired by a girl I knew called Lucy. A very county type. She and her boyfriend James were indulging in sadomasochist games and she changed and revelled in it. I want to explore what it is in the female psyche that wants to be the complete victim. When she sees a murder, she's excited. She decides not to escape because she likes her situation. She runs a garage and has the gun in one hand and the money in the other and she goes back to the boys because she likes it. I'd have kept the money and the gun – that's all a girl needs. This heroine has her vicious side. She makes a moral choice. I wrote this book when refugee hostels were being firebombed in Germany. I hope it's received as ironic. I'm using criticisms and flinging them back with irony.

Germaine Greer
She changed my life.
From Betty Walshe

Hillary Katzenell

"My father's family come from Brighton, so I'm sort of Brightonian. I was brought up in Scotland and Brighton and I was brought here to Brighton by the age of one to be with my father's family. After travelling around the country and being a career woman, I had a break in my career and I wondered where I would go to next and I thought that I might come to Brighton to give myself a half a chance of being comfortable. So that's how I came to Brighton, that was in the mid-seventies.

I am a book seller by profession and in 1990 I decided that I would describe myself as a retired book seller and move on to something else. I popped into the Brighton Voluntary Bureau and asked to look at the files of doing voluntary work and the Brighton Women's Centre came up and I thought, 'Oh, I'll go down there and see what it's all about,' and that was 1992 or 1993. I filled in one of the forms and then I got a call one day saying would I like to come down and be shown around. I went down and went in, upstairs, and the first thing that struck me was the amount of information that was available for women. It was quite extraordinary. The shelves and the walls were groaning with material and I thought to myself, I'll never know any of this, I'll never learn this, what use am I going to be down here? Somebody rang me asking would I like to come and so I started to work being a gate-keeper and phone answerer and somebody who was able to provide sources of information for women who came in. And that's what I did.

I did some fundraising for the Women's Centre and that was very small fry in comparison with what we are doing now. In fact, the lottery wasn't even available in those days. We thought that we would target women in Brighton, write them a letter and ask them if they felt like contributing and interestingly I think I managed to raise a thousand pounds, which was really quite good going considering that it was just local women and local funds.

We were always short of money, always. And we've always been seeking sources of funding. It's really hard work but somehow we managed to find three hundred pounds from some source to develop an idea about helping women who were on drugs. So I became a co-facilitator for the women's drug project which has now moved onto bigger and better things and is now called the Oasis project.

By this time it had been noted that in Brighton the Women's Aid project had been shut down, and the Brighton Women's Centre was deeply concerned about that. By this time I was still doing my rota work and we were getting a lot of domestic violence calls, three or four a week, and it was really disturbing, because there was just nowhere for them to go. We decided to write a letter to the Council in the strongest possible terms and demand some form of refuge or assistance for battered women.

Within a week or two, we were not only acknowledged but given quite a large sum of money from, I think it was, East Sussex County Council to resurrect or re-open the Women's Aid project. We ran it from the Women's Centre and we only had money for about three or four months. We started up and developed the Women's Aid project in the little back room which is now the counselling room of the Women's Centre. We managed to extract – I think it was from Brighton and Hove Council – some more money to continue the project for another few months and then we were given a big, big dollop of money and it was felt that we could offer up the post as a proper paid post around the country. This project has now become the Women's Refuge project.

I've done a few other bits and pieces; organising the arts festival, Taking Liberties, and lay-visiting at Brighton Police Station.

I feel very strongly that the Women's Centre should be a place for all women and should be acceptable to all women and I

Hillary Katzenell

Gerry Holloway
Because of her work in women's education. She is thoughtful, scholarly and a good friend with feminist principles. She is tireless in her encouragement of women seeking their education.
From Christine Zmroczek

Hillary Katzenell	think what we need to do is to look at ways in the future to attract all women and to understand that poverty is emotionally crippling as well as materially crippling. And yet at the same time it is these women who are poor, as it were, either emotionally or financially, who we want to attract, and in some way, empower.

Mimi Busby
She was a lovely mother who worked so hard to give my sister and me a loving, happy and secure childhood despite the many problems caused by the war, and she continued to do all she could for us throughout her life. I miss her.
From Mimi Blackwell

Jackie Cairns

Jackie has lived in Brighton all of her life. She married at 17 and has three children between the ages of 14 and six. She recently passed her driving test.

"I've always lived in Brighton, with my mum, dad and sister. I went to Kings Manor School. I didn't like school, I just wanted to leave, get married and have children. We lived in a bedsit in Blatchington Road, and got my first flat when James was born – my second boy, where we spent eleven years.

I've been married for fifteen years. I never had a good relationship with my mum and I would have liked a daughter.

Brighton was a good place when I was growing up, not so much now, it's changed a lot. My niece is thirteen and she was bullied in the park the other day, there wasn't all that when I was twelve or thirteen, I remember going to the pictures, and hanging around the arcades and it was safe, as safe as it could be. I don't feel that it is safe for my children to be doing that.

I like lots of girlie things, if I had a daughter, I would encourage her to do what she wanted to do. I'd have liked a little girl for all the frills and the lace and the girlie things. I

Kelle Kingsley
I first met Kelle at a time when I was making consequential changes to my life. Her friendship played a significant part in the person I am today.
From Lynne Fox

Jackie Cairns

think sometimes that's the sad bit about having boys because they are into football and rough things and I've never been one for standing there on a winter's day in the freezing cold, watching the boys play football. I think that I would have been more into a girl and whatever she wanted to do, I would have been there taking more interest I think.

Definitely no more children, I've got no more maternal feelings left whatsoever. Babies don't do anything for me at all. I was looking after a friend's baby for a couple of hours on a Thursday whilst she was going to college and I think that she wanted me to do it again but she hasn't asked me and I think she realises that it's not for me and it's not, mine are growing up and I don't want it on a regular basis, I don't mind every once in a while but I just haven't got the patience. No patience at all. It was really hard to have a baby in a bedsit, and when we moved into the flat it was just as tough having a baby, and James was just a toddler and it was hard work. It think that I had more patience with Jack – my third son – because I was older. I enjoyed him more as a baby. I was older and wiser. When you are younger you have dreams and I suppose mine was getting married and having children and living happily ever after and then you get to the age when you know it's never going to happen.

My greatest triumph? I don't think that there is one. It hasn't come yet, maybe it will come later on.

I think that you just stop thinking. It's just the kids and John. Everything goes out of the window and you get to the stage where you just don't know any more, you can't think and people say, what would you like to do or what would you have done and there isn't an answer I don't think – it's blank. Being a mum and a wife is all I've ever known and maybe it would have been different if I'd been more outgoing and made a life outside John and children when we first started off but I didn't, they were the be all and end all and it just stayed that way. I didn't lack confidence when I was younger, but now I do. It's just gone.

Jill Jones
The most unlikely yoga teacher in Brighton and Hove. No-one else could have made me take yoga seriously.
From Erica Smith

Jane

Jane has been living in Brighton for about thirty years.

"I'd been working in London for quite a while – I suppose about six or seven years, and things were getting a bit heavy with the police and stuff. You see they were very liberal for years – this was the 60s – but then the number of girls just exploded, and they had to be seen to be doing something about it towards the end of the 60s, and lots of girls started moving out of London. I'd heard about this great scene in Brighton, and I used to come down here for weekends a fair bit, so I thought it would be nice to live by the sea and I just packed my bags and went. I came down here with a girlfriend I'd made in London, but she's dead now – heroin abuse in Leeds – though I knew her here for about five years after we'd moved. Nice girl, but not very strong.

I wanted to ask you to say what it is you do for a living in your own terms.
You can call it anything you like really, I've heard it all.

But is there a word or phrase you prefer to use yourself?
I tell my clients that I'm a prostitute or a whore, they like the 'bad' words, although a few are little old men who like to say 'lady of the night' or 'familiar' or 'friend', quaint things like that. But you can use prostitute if you like – matter of fact, isn't it.

Yeah, OK. So, how did you get into prostitution?
Well, I've never been into anything much else, really! No, seriously, I wasn't into school, and I loved the sexual freedom of the 60s, and I was always popular with boys. I enjoy giving pleasure, and I needed some money, so I just drifted into it really. It wasn't such a big deal – a lot of girls I knew went into it from my area. I got my first client through sitting around in a café, and it was as casual as that for quite a while. When I came to Brighton, I got a bit more business-minded and started putting my cards around.

Do you think that Brighton is quite tolerant of prostitution?
Well, it is, yes, but then so are a lot of places really, if you look at it. As long as you're a decent, discreet sort of person and you don't aggravate anyone, you can pretty much do as you like. Of course, the seaside here is famous for dirty weekends and stuff, but most of my clients, well all of them now really, are regulars. Better that way – you know what you're dealing with.

Queenie
She is the most special and wonderful girl in the world.
From QC

Jane

Of course, you get trouble about cards in phone boxes, but I don't need to advertise anymore, and it was only ever just so the authorities could be seen to be upholding family values. I don't really get anyone's back up here as I keep myself to myself, work privately, and live in this district where we're all contained and safe. Everyone knows there are red-light areas, and as long as they can keep them at a distance but keep an eye on them, they're happy.

Would you say there was a community of prostitutes here?
Not really as far as I know, but I certainly know other prostitutes as friends, male and female, around here, as I don't get a lot of time to socialise, so you make friends on your doorstep. You get to be a good judge of character as a prostitute, and know who to trust.

Have you ever used the Women's Centre in Brighton?
No. I don't really use any of those community things, and I don't think I'd go down a bundle with the women down there! There's a lot of hostility from other women to prostitutes.

Is there anything you'd say to them, to defend your corner?
Just that I'm no rival for their territories – men can cut this sort of thing off from the women they love, and I'm just a physical release or someone to talk to. Men do want to do some pretty anti-social things, and a whore will do them when a wife is too busy trying to keep her family as socially accepted as possible. I think men and women have different sexual needs, and a lot of women would benefit from having a gigolo, but they cost much more 'cause women want all the time to come, and attention and love, whereas men can be in and out in ten minutes, and they don't mind me seeing other clients. But generally I'd say that the best thing to do is to keep out of their [women's] way or keep quiet. It's too emotional and you end up getting into an awful argument where you just can't say the right thing, or they end up walking off or pitying you as though you're too stupid to see what you're doing. I'd say to people who say I take money out of families that I would never encourage a family man to spend more than he can, 'cause some of these guys can get addicted to this, but in life there are things that happen whether you like it or not, and that you just have to try to ensure you don't do anything that makes it difficult to look in the mirror.

Have you ever had a pimp?
Not officially, no, but a recent boyfriend of mine got into thinking of himself like that and started to get shirty and demand money and stuff, so I got rid of him.

Have you suffered violence in prostitution?
Oh yes, but nothing I can't handle myself. I never get the police in or anything, and I screen people very carefully. There are always good, regular clients who are willing to fight off anyone for me if things go wrong. I have a couple of them on the memory buttons on my phone, so all I have to do is push one of those, and they know I need them if they 1471 it. I've had to pick up the pieces of some terrible scenes with some of the girls I know, but that's life for them, and they mostly take risks, which I'm really careful not to do. I've been very lucky in that respect I think, and I can be quite a tough nut myself if I need to be.

Do you think of doing anything else other than prostitution?
Well, I used to sometimes, when things were going badly, but I'm good at what I do, and it's a bit late now anyway! To be honest, I see myself doing this as long as I can now, as I've got enough to finish tomorrow. That's the thing with prostitution- it's very lucrative, and once you are in it, there's little opportunity to leave: you're kept very busy, believe me

What would you say are its main disadvantages?
Well obviously it's socially frowned on, and that's what really puts it down and makes it difficult to lead a normal life. Men can be bastards if you'll excuse my language, but I've also seen a lot of kindness. It isn't compatible with holding down a good relationship, and I've basically given up on that one. I couldn't have kids 'cause I've had so many abortions over the years and they took their toll. I've had STDs which can be very nasty indeed, but I haven't got AIDS, and I'm very careful to use protection now. I would never recommend prostitution to anyone – it's a lonely and a difficult life, but I can't regret my life – there are a lot of stories, a lot of things I've seen, and I've given a lot of happiness. I don't think my life was ever going to be simple, anyway.

Do you support legalisation of prostitution and state-run brothels?
That's a hard one. I think I change my mind a lot. In Amsterdam it seems to give the girls a fair bit of protection, but it's such a different set-up to mine, and I'm not sure it can really be compared. But if girls are in brothels, and the government is not too corrupt then I think it's a good way to control and keep clean what will always be there.

Have you ever been involved in the women's movement?
— No, not really my sort of thing. I sometimes think men are the oppressed ones – they are so at the mercy of their sex drives. Though I wouldn't tell them that!

Jane

Peggy Murray
She is a loving, supportive and tolerant person, who has never let me down and who enjoys life to the full – and I love her.
From Jen Murray

Jane

What about women's sex-drives?
Oh, I think they're there alright, they're just more tied into money factors, and building a home, or protection, or whatever. Not so much just for their own sake.

What do you think of the idea of a women-only space?
I'm not surprised there is one – it's always good to be with people you've got something in common with. There are loads of men-only spaces aren't there. I'd have thought it would encourage lesbianism, though, once everyone discusses how much men annoy them, and how beautiful and strong some women are. Nothing wrong with that, but my policy is to get on with living with them and accept them as they are. Well it's not just my policy – it's my job!

Jean Hopkins

Jean was born in Birmingham and came to Brighton in 1995 after leaving the Czech Republic where she was teaching English to personnel in an aircraft company.

"When I first arrived in Brighton, I'd heard about the Women's Centre, but I'd never found it as I was quite new to Brighton. And I am quite grateful that I didn't, because in those days transsexuals weren't accepted and I was going through a very, very heavy time and I needed the support. What introduced me to the Women's Centre was they were discussing the acceptance of transsexuals into the Centre and I felt that this was one way I could help, so that's what introduced me.

I didn't choose to be a woman, in a sense I have had to accept what has been shouting at me since the earliest age, unfortunately when you are a child you don't have much choice in what way people treat you. Because I looked physically like a boy I was expected to be like a boy but it made me very isolated, I have always been a loner which is sad, I don't want to be a loner, which causes difficulties

Anne Nyssen
Welder, activist, free spirit, feet on the ground, head in the clouds, Belgian feminist, woman lover.
From Margaretta Jolly

Jean Hopkins

Melita
For being an infamous woman of Brighton.
From Anonymous

nowadays. It's one of the things now that I have settled down and accepted who I felt I was before, the water gets even murkier because people have a certain ignorance about what a transsexual is or what their sexuality is or whether you are supposed to be guarded against certain things, is it catchable and is this another form of homosexuality? I am not a homosexual in the sense that I like my own gender, so if you like, I don't like women as partners.

Coming originally from Birmingham and as the old saying goes, when you go north amongst the snow and cold the warmer the heart gets. People tend to be a lot more sociable and a lot more open about themselves, and the further you go south, the more cultured or affluent, and the more difficult it is for people to show themselves how they are. People down south tend to open up the more that you get to know them, but I think that they still have their guards up.

I didn't choose this, because I would have ended up dead, because of the difficulty of even getting treatment or medical help, I almost threw myself under a bus. And I did at one point shoot myself, because I had run out of hope. But oddly enough it wasn't because I wanted to die, when I said shoot myself I was shooting at my genitals, I didn't see myself as wanting to die. So it was an end, it wasn't a resignation to life. When I wanted to chuck myself under a bus, I didn't do it and that was the positive side to me, I have to put my life to some use for the future if you like, I don't want my life to be of no use.

I had always been quiet and reserved. When I left school that was my freedom, my time to explore, to find out what the heck I was. And so I had various jobs and in one of them I did encounter a homosexual, and that wasn't me. I didn't get involved because I had more important things to find myself. And so in 1969 I emigrated to Australia and there I started to delve into the Chinese culture because I thought that was a deeper more understanding society and started to learn Cantonese, got involved with the Chinese community and fortunately or unfortunately my teacher, Chinese teacher, was a Christian. She got me involved with the Chinese church in Australia. So then I started to study Christianity and almost went to theological college but just like most religions the issue of sexuality comes up and there is no denying that the church has a problem with that.

My philosophy and understanding at that point was deeper than what I felt Christianity was and I started going to Buddhism and that offered more promise. What Buddhism was saying was, look into yourself and accept yourself for what you are. And there came a crisis point and out of the blue the book

Jean Hopkins

Conundrum by Jan Morris, came out, which actually answered all the questions I had been asking. This was 1975 then so I decided that I then had to come back home and say 'hey Dad' – Mum had died, unfortunately two years earlier – but Dad was still alive and I thought 'great I can go home now and start finding all the solutions.'

Sadly Dad died the day that I left Australia and I didn't hear about it until the ship arrived in Panama, so when I did arrive back both of my parents had demised and I couldn't really talk to my sister about it, although she was one of the few members of my family to understand, who I keep in touch with and talk to. She had married by then and her husband couldn't cope with this at all. It was difficult to find anyone who appreciated what transsexuality was but I managed to see a doctor, I had read about psychiatry and I was feeling very nervous and my doctor said, I can't help you but I will make you an appointment with a psychiatrist and of course this was like meeting the devil incarnate and I felt sure that this person didn't accept transsexuality so that wasn't much help and that was when the difficulties started, because I couldn't find the solution.

I got involved in counselling and my counsellor got in touch with the Brook Advice clinic and they got me in touch with a doctor at Guys. I had heard of Randall from *Conundrum* and I had got an appointment with him at Charing Cross. I had never cross-dressed before and I had heard that you had to live in the role for quite a while. So the first time I actually went out dressed as a woman was to catch a train to get to London, Charing Cross.

I had very little money, got to London, got out the train, Charing Cross Hospital wasn't in Charing Cross it was in Hammersmith and I hadn't got the fare to get there so I literally had to walk there and half way there my toes had pushed their way through my tights and I had to take them off and by the time I got there I was extremely tired and Dr Randall turned around and said that he couldn't help me. I was devastated.

I spent a year at a Buddhist Monastery at Sussex and eventually found the Richmond Fellowship, I was a resident there and the doctor said that she would help me and start giving me hormones which was the first step, so to speak. Fortunately Professor Watson at Guys agreed that he would help me and even then eleven years ago you had to work and live full time as a woman for two years, so it was still quite a difficult ordeal. And even though I couldn't find work, I did voluntary work for MIND and went in there every day and so he accepted that, so after seeing him for four years I then got

Linda Pointing
A Brighton Woman who has worked tirelessly to promote gay and lesbian issues for many years. As a sister lesbian I feel grateful for all that Linda for her ceaseless effort in ensuring we have a voice.
From Jean Wooller

Jean Hopkins

my operation. But even then the cut backs started and put in doubt if the NHS would fund the operation. Eventually I got my operation in 1986 but unfortunately that prolapsed so I had to go in again to have the prolapse fixed, which has never turned out successful, but I thought my problems would stop as soon as I had my operation, that I wouldn't have these male hormones flowing through my body.

I am still struggling against those same issues, such as electrolysis. I realised then, that because I had had such a difficult childhood, I was a loner, I was constantly needled and that at one point I had actually had needles jabbed into me, so having electrolysis would bring up these emotions in me and to this day it still does. I have heard about laser treatment, but there is no NHS help for laser treatment. My facial features are quite masculine, I have a large nose, and because of the lack of electrolysis, a large chin and I still have an Adam's Apple, so I have all these things to solve. And to compound things when I started hormones, my breasts didn't just grow, they grew and grew and grew and grew, literally around my navel, but that was OK, in fact it was only four weeks ago that I was able to get a breast reduction. Now I have a reasonable bust, before I couldn't find anything to wear, I couldn't wear the fashion and you get some weird people who want to know you as well, you know you think that they are nice people, but they have got their own hidden agendas and that's another encounter that has made my life a lot more difficult. Especially people who say 'they're false aren't they?' Like I am doing this just for some quirk in personality. It's sad. This is the thing about allowing people to know you and that over time all those fears and anxieties pass but it's having, knowing, being, in a social environment you get to know people. I am starting to meet people, even after three years but I find this resistance in people to be open and honest very difficult and I am still alone, I haven't met anyone yet.

Life is like standing on the bank watching the river go by and you have to grab whatever comes down the river. Once it's past you've lost it and there's been so many things that have passed by that I've lost that I just hope that I'm alert enough to see whatever comes down the river next.

Jen Murray

Jen came to Brighton from Edinburgh in 1970 and was one of the founding members of Brighton Women's Centre and Brighton Women's Aid.

"When I first got to Brighton there wasn't a Women's Centre. I'd always felt angry because things didn't make sense to me, didn't feel right. I was out on a limb because I never wanted to do all of the sort of things women were supposed to do... I thought it was me, you know, I thought it was me who had the problem.

One of the women where I worked knew about this thing called 'women's lib' and there were meetings in Brighton. We both thought, 'wow, perhaps this could be for us'. We were a bit nervous, but we went along. It was in a café in Hove in Westbourne Gardens, with a group of women sitting around and talking about women's liberation, the Women's Liberation Movement as it was called then. There had been a conference in 1970, and they drew up the four demands of the Women's Liberation Movement. It was equal pay... free contraception and abortion on demand... 24-hour nurseries... and equal education and opportunities. So those were the four demands that anybody who got involved in the movement would accept and work towards.

So, when we got to this café in Hove, we were discussing what we could do about all these various things. There were a lot of women involved, you know, a lot of energy, a lot of different kinds of women, older women, younger women, a lot of students obviously, because they always were the backbone of the movement in Brighton, but a lot of local Brighton women, and women working like me as well. It was wonderful.

When you came into the movement you joined a 'consciousness-raising' group – a CR group – which was like a small encounter group where women got together and talked about their experiences. It was quite structured, the CR groups, and you remembered the women in your CR group like the women you might have gone to university with. We wanted to get out and do something – we had this anger. We'd heard about Erin Pizzey and Chiswick Women's Aid, so my particular CR group thought, if it happens in London, it must be happening in Brighton. So we did some local research, and talked to the police and Social Services and housing and all

Ilse Singer
– who got interested in radical feminism in her late 60s, was involved in the first days of the Brighton Women's Centre and who can forget her women's parties?
From Margaretta Jolly

Jen Murray

sorts, and we decided, my group, that we would work towards setting up a Women's Aid Refuge. There were other women who wanted to set up a Women's Centre.

Running up to '74, we were looking for premises and money and what-have-you. And as it happened Social Services at that time had some empty properties, on Buckingham Road. They didn't have the money to develop them so they were offering them to local groups to use until they could develop them themselves. We liaised with the community worker and it ended up that we got them, four houses, those sort of tall houses, two for Women's Aid and two for the Women's Centre next door which was very handy. So the Women's Lib group then started meeting in the Women's Centre, it was used for all sorts of things. There was a rota of women keeping it open, pregnancy tests, meeting space and information. It was never terribly well organised, as you can imagine.

Women's Aid was developing in the two houses next door and used the Women's Centre as a referral point because it was quite a good cover – we could say it was a Women's Centre and nobody knew, certainly to start with, that there was actually a refuge next door as well. It got a bit well known over the years but we moved to a different house in the end.

When Social Services actually took their premises back, then Women's Aid and the Women's Centre diverged a bit. Women's Aid went off to better premises and the Women's Centre was a little bit nomadic for a while. For a while we were actually operating from a flat in Moulsecoomb – a local woman councillor let us use a room in her flat to work from, so it meant geographically we were actually very near all those working class women that we had always said we wanted to attract into the movement but who had never really wanted to come and join!

The Centre was only in Moulsecoomb briefly, then it went to Brighton and Hove Resource Centre in North Road until that building burnt down – the PACT building was built on top of the rubble. From there it went to Marlborough Place, and at this point I didn't really have any more contact with it because I'd started to get involved with my own career and with Women's Aid, that was my particular interest.

Throughout the 70s the Women's Movement was strongest, it was only towards the end of the 70s that it really began to split. It was quite a big split between, very crudely, on the one hand, women who were radical feminists who considered there was no way forward in terms of having any kind of relationships with men, and on the other hand, socialist feminists who considered that feminism couldn't be seen in isolation from

Jen Murray

other politics, like socialism. So there was this fragmentation from about the late 70s.

What I really miss is those days in the 70s when there was such a big group of women involved in all sorts of things… the abortion campaign was very strong in Brighton, a lot of the women in Brighton were involved in marches and helped with the organisation. Reclaim the Night, all those marches in Brighton, you name it – whatever came out of the Women's Liberation Movement, Brighton was there, because it was one of the strongest places. There was a series of Sexuality Conferences which talked about all aspects of sexuality – lesbianism, heterosexuality, bi-sexuality, orgasms, whatever. We were very broad in terms of our interests and that's what I miss. I can't divorce the Women's Centre from the Women's Lib Movement as a whole because that's my history.

So what is the future of the Women's Movement? I think it is that women are involved in different areas, like I work now, my interest is the Women's Management Network, which is not particularly a feminist organisation, although there are women like me within it who are feminists. And then other people want to do things like the Women's Centre and other people again want to do Women's Aid so it does seem to have fragmented.

I think politically, socially, culturally we've still got loads of opportunities to expand our potential and our possibilities. And there's still lots of women who although they've been born and brought up post-women's liberation, still get beaten up by their husbands. All those things are still happening, so yes, there's still lots of room for change and progress.

The 70s was a continuous high point, there was so much going on. The initial high point was finding a group of women who felt the same things as I did and meant that I didn't feel such a weirdo and it wasn't my personal pathology but it was something wrong with society. Another high point was getting the premises for Women's Aid and the Women's Centre and actually having something concrete to work with. We got money for that as well, we didn't just get the premises. Women's Aid was the first project in Brighton ever to get an Urban Aid grant, that was a high point.

The fact that we were doing it for ourselves as a relatively small group meant enormous repercussions: the Equal Pay Act, the Sex Discrimination Act, the very formal changes and things like the abortion campaign, the Women's Aid Refuge, just the general ambience. It was actually a very limited number of women who produced those amazing changes – I think I'd say that the women who were involved were doing it for themselves.

Wendy Savage
– the consultant obstetrician who dared to challenge the masculinst assumptions and practices of the male orthodoxy in insisting that women in childbirth should be accorded dignity, respect and choice.
From Paula Colbran

From the Brighton Women's Centre archive, 1988

Joyce Edmond-Smith

"I was on the periphery [of the Women's Centre] in 1974. I was at Sussex University and I was part of the women's group there and the Women's Centre was part of what we were arguing for, and that was in a way the extent of my involvement. I'd go down to Marlborough Place occasionally. At the time I was more involved with women's education and training, which was my area really, and still is.

My involvement deepened when I got involved in politics in the Labour Party. I joined the Labour Party in 1981 and really got very involved there in the women's section, and the women's section at the time was quite a controversial issue. There were views that having special women's sections was divisive and it was more middle class women doing their thing. On the other hand all of the arguments about the women's movement, about discrimination, about power, were being taken into the Labour Party by people who had been in the Women's Movement and were moving into politics.

Joyce Edmond-Smith

Then I became a Councillor in 1986. The debate within the women's section at the time within the Labour party had been this question of spaces for women and that was very much what we had been fighting for. When we won the 1986 election we had in our manifesto the setting up of a Women's Committee. When we got the Women's Officer, Brenda Wilkinson, one of the things we immediately set about doing was looking at the structures; one was the workplace nursery, the other was the Women's Centre.

The Women's Centre already had had a grant from the Council. One of the things the Women's Committee did was to stabilise the issue of funding for the Women's Centre. It was because of the Women's Committee that the Women's Centre eventually moved here. It was absolutely essential that it move out of Marlborough Place, it just wasn't appropriate. That support has continued with ups and downs along the way. Ever since we were in power we have had a situation of cuts.

The other crucial thing that happened at that time was the development of a voice for ethnic minority women in the town. What the Women's Committee did was we had co-optees, we had a co-optee always from the Women's Centre and tried to identify women from the ethnic minority communities and co-opt them on. Over the years we managed to bring in ethnic minority women, but what was most important was the way that the women who came onto the committee just… developed. We've now got a Hindu Women's Group, a Sudanese Women's Group. Until then they were completely invisible in the town.

The other thing was that we had our very first International Women's Day held in the Women's Centre in 1987. We came into power in 1986 and thought, what can we do, how can we launch this idea of women in the town? and we came up with a celebration of International Women's Day. That has just got bigger and better every year and indeed the following year it was completely done by ethnic minority women. The first year it was largely the Women's Committee that pushed it.

The big question still for women in education, is older women, the question of access, what LAUNCH is doing really. What seems to be happening is a kind of aggravation of the differences which were always there – call them class differences if you like. A group of women who are more confident and will probably do better. The class thing is becoming more exacerbated in the education of women. Young women who don't see a future, who haven't got the kind of backing, they're the ones we need to be paying attention to, and the older women. I teach on an Access Course – it's such a

Nina West
– who campaigned for one parent families.
From Shirley West

Joyce Edmond-Smith classic story – women who left school early, had their first child then did part-time work, then the marriage has gone wrong, or sometimes just the children are in school and they think, 'I want to do something better than this'. It's absolutely crucial that we keep open those avenues of return and facilitate this – it's been an uphill struggle – the question of childcare is still unresolved.

We've got to hang onto the possibility of choice. All my life I've been involved in getting women into education and training, therefore into work, and I've argued for 24-hour childcare. Now I find myself saying, wait a minute, for those women who don't want to, who want to be at home with their children, they ought to have that choice. We shouldn't be saying, we can't support you, you're costing too much money, that is not the appropriate message.

The Women's Centre can be much more a part of the mainstream of what is going on in Brighton. There's going to be an interesting question arising about age, and whether youngish women feel there is a need for a 'women only' space. I suspect they will feel it when trouble happens. Consciousness-raising usually happens when there is a problem. You go and talk to other women and find that, 'hey, it's not only me'. I think that's probably where the role of the Women's Centre lies. It is, in some respects, a haven.

I think the attitudes are changing but cultural change is slow and is very much affected by power relations and I haven't seen any evidence yet that we've really got those power issues sorted. [Sexism] is not dead, but it is changing, it's becoming more subtle, more flexible, more confused, more diverse. Maybe the big issues of the future are going to be children and how as a society we care for and look after our children and that necessarily raises the relationship between men and women.

Judy Richards

Judy came to Brighton 20 years ago as a student. She studied a degree in computing, but got very involved in the Students Union and decided she preferred politics to studying.

In 1987 I got involved in the Women's Centre. Where I particularly got involved was when they were looking to move from Marlborough Place into other premises in St George's Mews. Having to lug this huge electric cooker up the stairs with two other women, laying down carpets because one person knew how to do it and the rest of us would just do as we were told! Putting adverts on a radio phone-in asking for different items of office equipment. Trying to put in computers. I could see the need for women to have access to computers to be able to do things like newsletters and things like that. A couple of us got involved in a computer sub-group, looking at what we needed and where we would get the funding from. We managed to get the money, and managed to get a fairly basic computer for those days. Other women from the computer industry got involved so it expanded from there.

After helping the Women's Centre to start up I also got involved in NALGO. By the summer of 1988, I realised I'd been

Annette Davis
Thank you for your overwhelming support and unquestioningly belief in me.
From Natalie Matos

Judy Richards

I didn't use the Women's Centre at Marlborough Place. Things can have an open-door policy, but it's not always as welcoming as people might want it to be. I think sometimes Black women, if you're walking in and it's a sea of white faces, or just one or two white faces, how those one or two white faces react to you can make a difference as to whether you go back again. And worse – whether you tell anybody you know about whether or not you think they should go there or not. Sometimes it didn't feel as friendly as it could have done, and it might have been that people weren't sure how to deal with a Black face walking through the door, but it shouldn't really have made much difference.

involved in the Alton abortion bill, the Section 28 campaign and I'm sure there was another equalities campaign in Winter 87–88, on a regional basis down in Sussex/Surrey/Kent. So in the summer of 1988, the national conference for the whole of NALGO happened to be in Brighton, so I just went in to see what was going on. I found people I had been at college with ten years before. I got involved again in Women's, Black, Lesbian & Gay, Disability and District Equal Opportunities activities, and actually got onto the National Black Members Committee.

On and off I was on the National Women's Committee as well, sometimes as a regional representative, sometimes as a representative from the Black Members Committee. Having some of the battles with NALGO and then with UNISON, that we'd been trying to work through in society and maybe naively assumed that as this was our Union, they must know how to do this. But finding that in some ways there was more ignorance and resistance there than you might get from people that you might meet in the town hall or police station.

We tried on a number of occasions to get them to look at the suitability of the crèche, not just for Black women but for lesbians and disabled parents. The images that the children had from the toys and games that they were playing with, the sort of workers that they used, didn't really have an idea of equal opps. I don't think the Committee was able or willing to take ownership of equal opportunities to that kind of degree. What brought it to a head was the last year of NALGO which would have been the winter of 1992. One of the women who happened to be on the Black Members Committee had come with her three daughters, one of whom had Sickle Cell Anaemia. She'd put on her form that she had Sickle Cell Anaemia and that therefore they needed to be aware of what the symptoms were, of what a sign of a crisis might be, so they could catch her quickly and get her to hospital if need be, because it's a life threatening illness. Nobody in the crèche enquired about it until she brought her to the crèche when they asked her what Sickle Cell was, and they said, 'oh well, it's alright, we've got Black workers, they'll deal with it.'

I was actually on the National Black Members Committee for ten years. I came in when there was a struggle going on about whether there should even be a Black Members Committee, and whether it should be Black only, which for me was absolutely basic. There is no way you can have a Black Members Committee that isn't Black only. But within a lot of unions it is an issue. It is the Black members who are a threat. They don't know many Black people. It's about power, and they assume that having self-organised groups, is about us wanting to take power from them.

Judy Richards

Usually white, heterosexual able-bodied men. Even in UNISON where 70% of the membership is women, they have not managed to get across the board from the National Executive Council to delegations to the TUC Congress.

I had friends who were anarchists, which I thought was interesting. I was totally disillusioned with the SWP (Socialist Workers Party) and the Anti-Nazi League stuff. Most of the people down here who were involved in the SWP seemed to be middle-class students having three years out of being middle-class and trying to tell me, who was definitely working-class, what it was like to be working-class just because they put on a pair of DM's, a donkey jacket and adopted an accent for a couple of years! Knowing full well that once they'd done their degrees they'd go back to mummy and daddy and get nice jobs earning a lot more than I'd ever have the opportunity of earning because I was truly working-class.

So anarchism seemed much more democratic, if a lot more disorganised at times! A lot of the things that I remember people being involved in were not particularly legal so I can't begin to talk about them. But there was a protest against banks and the arms trade. I think it was the Metropole Hotel used to have an annual arms fair, and there were lots of people who used to meet and picket that. I remember actions against banks when people used to go out and spray paint the banks, particularly Barclays Bank because of the involvement in the arms trade, and in South Africa.

The most fun thing we used to do was the trolley actions. We'd pick a day, usually a Saturday, go to a supermarket and load up trolleys with all South African produce, take them to the checkout, sometimes half a dozen separate trolleys, so every check out would be occupied, and once they had rung up all the items we would give them a leaflet saying 'This is a protest against South Africa. These are South African goods and we're not paying for them'. Knowing the till would be snarled up while they took off all the items. Somebody did get arrested once for denting a tin, but it didn't get very far! I don't know how much good it did but I think Tesco's was one of the first to stop stocking South African produce, so it must have added to the other pressure to achieve a result. I think the people on the tills thought it was hilarious because I suppose it was a change to their day.

I haven't had to do it for a while but there have been occasions when I've been walking through town and someone makes a racist comment and I will just shout at them 'Eff off, you racist', or whatever, and then think what does everybody else think, but then I don't care. It makes me feel better not to

Hannah Hurst
For loving women and sharing her knowledge freely but most of all, for breaking all the rules – it was worth it.
From Kelle Kingsley

Judy Richards

Brighton is a bit more of a multi-racial town now than when I first came here, but not a lot. It used to be the Black people you knew were probably students. If you didn't know them by name you knew them by sight. Nowadays you can walk through the town and you may never have seen them before and you may never see them again for months. What sort of support people get I don't know. There are more groups now than there were. There are more clubs than there were but they seem to move around.

let something like that go. I know a lot of people who bottle it up and don't respond to it, who then are just scared stiff of walking out the front door. I won't let that happen to me.

That is also one of the reasons I took an industrial tribunal against Brighton Council. Although I'd not finished the computing degree, I'd gone on and got another qualification which would allow me to work myself up. I'd applied for a whole range of jobs and not got anywhere. Quite often it was the case that over the telephone they were really keen, I was exactly the sort of person they were looking for. It's not as good on Equal Opportunities employment, the computer industry, as others.

There was one occasion which sealed it for me, where there was somebody who had been incredibly enthusiastic over the telephone, as I walked in the door, the first time they realised I was Black, their hand was up to shake my hand, and as I walked in the hand's not coming forward enough for me to be able to shake it! They were so surprised that I was actually Black. I think, as in a lot of companies they realised that if you bring in a Black person who has got these skills, at some point you're going to have to promote them, over the heads of white people who may not like taking instructions. 'They may one day be a challenge to my job. Better keep them out'.

So I decided to get a job in a large company that has a computer section as opposed to an actual computer company, and move on. I tried other statutory bodies and didn't get very far, and then a job came up at Brighton Council which was so much what I was already doing in terms of voluntary work that I thought, 'well I've got to have a good chance at this one'. One of the things they wanted was computing skills, information and computing. There were not that many people around with as much experience as me, campaigning and information skills.

They decided to re-advertise it because they somehow decided after the initial responses that computing wasn't an essential criteria, and that didn't worry me very much but it did seem a bit odd. I had another job offer so I needed to know what they had decided after the second lot of interviews from the second advert. Because I couldn't get a straight answer out of them I took the other job.

I found out who had got the Brighton Council job. The woman obviously had skills but we had discussed it before the interviews and she had expressed to me privately that she wouldn't have bothered applying if she had known I was applying. I had ten or eleven years experience, I had produced newsletters, handbooks and stuff. I really couldn't see how she could have had so much experience to match mine, being virtually fresh out of university. I put in a race relations

Judy Richards

questionnaire, and then I heard nothing. I ended up having to put in a tribunal application. I knew about the job going to somebody else at the end of January 1990, and I still couldn't get any straight answers out of them by the summer after the tribunal application was logged. The tribunal had to be adjourned two or three times because they refused to show me application forms for other applicants for example. The longer they delayed the more suspicious I got. I think it was about 15 months after I decided I needed to do something about it that it came to tribunal.

At the tribunal they were not as honest as they should have been. Their reasons why the other person had got the job were so blatantly not true. So the tribunal had no choice but to find against them. For me it was important. I ran the case myself, with someone to represent me on the day. I proved to myself my skills and abilities. I think there have only been about three successful race discrimination cases in Brighton. I think there comes a time when you can't just keep complaining about the things that happen to you, you have to do something about it.

I think it's one of the reasons why the Black Women's Group that has just celebrated its tenth anniversary is very important. The Group is based in Brighton although we have members from Brighton and Hove, Lewes, Peacehaven and Newhaven area. In the early days it was very much women coming together giving support. Some of us had been involved on the Women's Centre rota, and thought 'well where is the Black Women's Group, where is the Black Women's Network?' So we thought let's have a meeting.

We started with half a dozen women and the mailing list got up to 30 before I stopped counting. In the early days it was very much coming together to share experiences about being Black, so things that you'd gone through, positive images, body image, mixed relationships and things that you wouldn't be able talk about anywhere else. There were some women who'd been at university who knew each other quite well, others who'd met through work or socially. Women felt comfortable talking. A lot of professional women, a lot of them working outside Sussex. I think it was sometimes a shock that any subject that came up where they wanted a view from Black people, the Black Women's Group could give you a view. Some of us were involved in a national level with race politics, either in community networks or trade unions, or just from knowing people that were involved in things like that.

We started in October 1988, and round about November 1988 the Law Centre had its AGM, and it was talking about race issues so we went along. Maybe the only other Black person was the

Kelle Kingsley
For her friendship, support, generosity and inspiration to me as an adult.
From Bunty Dann

Judy Richards

speaker. He was one of the local Black community leaders. One of the things he said was that when people were racially harassed they moved them. We thought that that seemed a bit odd. I said 'Why do you move the people that are being harassed? Why don't you prosecute the people that are harassing them?'. You would think that was obvious. There was this sort of stunned silence and they had to be forced to have a discussion of our experience of harassment and the need for support. They agreed to have another meeting to discuss that.

From an innocent comment and support from other people knowing the law better than me, we've got a Racial Harassment Forum, where we have a better time, on paper, in the way that police record incidents and train officers, than other areas do. The Forum includes the police. Education is very active again, Social Services are quite active, and obviously community groups are involved. Obviously after eight or nine years you get quiet periods where people lose direction or aren't quite sure what's going on. We've had to re-focus, to look again at what's going on. A new government, the Stephen Lawrence campaign, and there is much more awareness. The police seem really concerned about their image, and when people ask questions they are really keen to come up with the answers.

One year 25% of the incidents were on one particular estate. We thought that was possibly because a lot of the Sudanese refugees had been housed within a short period of time on that estate which might have proved to be a catalyst for what was going on anyway. We tried looking for national guidance but couldn't find any. A lot of organisations have policy documents and posters, but it was finding what to do beyond that.

It was at this stage that we decided the Group had to rethink itself. We had somebody come to a meeting who was a member of one of the Black community groups. She'd had years of abuse within her privately owned block of flats. When works were needed doing hers was the last to be done or didn't get done at all, so there was obviously something going on. She had been to most of the organisations that sat around the Racial Harassment Forum table and got nowhere with them. So I think it was the embarrassment of her saying, 'Well I went to your organisation and this is what they did', that people thought that we needed to get some training. We need to get back to basics and decide what we're doing. So we've now split into two groups. There's a policy section that looks at what policies we've got and how they're working. We've re-designed the racial harassment form, so people are going to be trained in that.

Organisations are being asked to send three people maximum to get training in that, so people will know how to

Jean Calder
Her openness to others and generosity of spirit, even to those who opposed her (inside and outside Brighton Labour Party in the late 80s/ early 90s), provided a model for me of what co-operative, democratic, community politics might be.
Anon

Judy Richards

fill out the form, why it's important to fill out the form, and where the form goes to. So we can have a database where we can identify any existing patterns and trends more quickly and decide if there's a particular area to target. And I'm sure there are some bits around certain pubs, certain parts of town, where there is more going on than anywhere else. It may just be because there are more people around and therefore things will happen. But if nothing else, to have posters up as you see in other boroughs, saying 'Racial Harassment is not acceptable. Report it, don't put up with it', that would make a difference.

I think I have become infamous over the years! Especially with the industrial tribunal there are people certainly within the Council who are aware of who I am at meetings and stuff. They are almost expecting me to sprout another head! Because of the union activity a lot of people do know me, and other campaigns.

I'm very involved in my work, I work for Sussex Racial Equality Council. One of those voluntary organisations that can end up taking over your life. I'm also the lead case worker, so I take cases of racial discrimination. You never know from one day to the next how much energy it will require. You sometimes have to learn legislation as you're going along. There isn't time to get involved in other campaigns, but then it goes in phases and at the moment there aren't campaigns going on, it seems to be very quiet. Maybe some people are relying on the Labour party to fix everything.

There are a lot more Black groups and Black women's groups around. There's a lot of interchange of information and ideas, so we have a more cohesive community but we still don't have access to the resources. But a lot of things I can sit here and say that it's been activity from the Black Women's Group that have led to changes in the Council. It may have been that those people saw it as the next career move for them, but at the end of the day we have had the chances of sitting around the tables and consulting. There is race equality training where there wasn't before, and I know that the Black Women's Group and other forums were really involved in asking for the training. We knew enough people that were trainers to make it into something. It's never as good as you think it should be, and it's always somebody who doesn't understand enough who is organising it but things have moved on. There's still a lot to do. If they were as receptive as the police often are with things like this, I think we would have moved a lot further by now.

My first general election as an adult was when Mrs Thatcher was elected. I hadn't got my act together to get my vote transferred, or a postal vote, so I felt really guilty. I thought it was my fault that she'd got in!!

Bettina Klaubert
You didn't make it across the divide.
From Geraldine Primarolo

Julia Reddaway

"I came down to Brighton in 1986 after deciding that I wanted to have a baby. It wasn't possible to do that in London and I couldn't carry on working in London as I couldn't afford a house there. Bernard, my husband, and I both decided that Brighton was a place that we knew and we liked. I had a brother down here and we literally chucked in everything, sold up and moved down to Brighton.

I run LAUNCH, a women's training at the Brighton Women's Centre which aims to improve the employment prospects of disadvantaged women. It came about because one of the women from the Women's Centre had put a bid in to the Council for Single Regeneration Budget money, and I was appointed as co-ordinator in January 1997. I support women through an eight-week induction programme which gives them career guidance and advice and helps them to set a personal goal of what they want to do, what sort of work they want to do and which qualifications they want to work towards. The programme also has a lot of confidence building techniques built in to it. So women go through that programme, then enrol at college and work towards a qualification and wherever possible I help them to get some work experience placements, into employment or higher education, and that's been running now for two years.

Julia Reddaway

Do you feel strongly about having a women only space in Brighton?

I do – I think it's very important for a lot of women to have that. I did an evaluation after a whole group of about 50 women had been on the project and one of the things that I asked them was how important it was that the project has been run thorough the Brighton Women's Centre and every single respondent said that it was very important to them. I think that there is a need for having, being in, an environment where it is women only, where women can talk and share problems and difficulties, with a feeling that it's confidential.

Has the LAUNCH project been such a success?

I think the women who have stuck with it have gained for a number of reasons. Their confidence has been boosted enormously, and again that was something that came up on the evaluation I did, everybody felt more confident, more equipped for work and in the vast majority of cases they have gained a qualification. For some of them it was the first qualification that they have ever, ever had. I think that those who have had children have benefited from time away from their children and losing that sense of isolation and having something to talk about other than babies nappies. They have made new relationships and made new friends, they have found themselves in a supportive environment where they know that if they don't turn up for a class one day, for example, half a dozen people are going to phone them up to check that they are OK. And just the feeling that they are progressing, they are going somewhere. Some of the comments and letters are from women saying that this has completely changed their lives. So in that respect I think that the project has been enormously successful.

Do you think that having a child is seen as having negative connotations, that you are only in society if you are actually working? So in effect equality has won us the right to raise our children and have to work and be superwomen?

I think that women do feel under pressure to be all things to everybody whereas in the past if they had a provider, their role was keeping the house, raising the children. I think that's a dilemma for women, and for men as well. I think that part of the answer is for men to take more responsibility as a parent and that can only really happen if employers recognise the needs and responsibilities of both parents and treat them equally. An awful

Rosemary Lovatt
I'd like her (among others, of course!) to be thanked for the frequently thankless task of keeping the Women's Centre going for so many years, with her customary common sense and good humour. Cheers, Rosemary!
From Liz Williams

Julia Reddaway

lot has got to change before men and women can both work, both bring up children and be treated completely equally.

What's been your personal experience of discrimination as a woman?

Perhaps I have been very lucky, although I am sure that I am not unique, but I've never felt that I've not been promoted because I was a woman; I have tended to work in organisations or industries which are fairly female dominated. I have worked in women's publishing for example. I've worked with a lot of women so perhaps that's one of the reasons, but I feel, personally, that I've always been promoted or rewarded because of my abilities or not rewarded because of my lack of abilities, and I have never ever once felt that I have been discriminated against in the work place. I think that it would be very difficult I'm sure, for example, if I was in the very male dominated professions.

You have a daughter, how do you think her life will be, will it be different to yours?

I think that it will be more difficult. I think my daughter will not find it as easy as I have really. I think that it will be a much more competitive world for her and that she will face difficulties that I haven't faced but I don't think that she will find it difficult because she'll be a woman, and I am glad that I've got a daughter and not a son because I would be far more worried about a son's future prospects now than I would about women. I think that women are going to be the major work force in the future and that the skills that are required, not only in this country, but world wide tend to be more communicative skills, which women, I think, are better at than men. We will never have full employment, and by the time she is going into the labour market the whole world will be very different. And I think that it will be a challenging time. I worry about the environment, I worry about her health, I think that if she has a child, will her children be able to breath the air. I see a huge number of women who are in their late 40s–50s who may perhaps be recently divorced, whose children have grown up and left home. They have so many talents and so much to offer, but no one wants them because there is definitely a real problem with ageism, which strikes me as one of the most ludicrous reasons for not employing people. Older people have had experience, a greater understanding of life and often make the most reliable employees. They have more to give, they have a greater understanding of a lot of needs and they are very motivated. And it think that there is a whole group of women who are really being very hard done by because of some employers' very narrow minded attitude towards older people.

Lucy Johnson
For her unconditional support and friendship over many years
From Julia Reddaway

Linda Pointing

"I've been in Brighton itself since 1976 but I was born just along the coast in Shoreham. I lived there for nineteen years before I went away to university. I was a student in Hull for three years, spent three years in the London suburbs, then I came home and I've been here ever since.

I made good friends in London with some lesbians who took me under their wing. I was still a novice dyke. I'd had several relationships with women but I'd never ventured onto the scene. They took me to clubs and discos and taught me to drink five pints of beer a night. When I came down to Brighton they made sure I'd got a copy of *Gay News* which had listings in the back of all the clubs and pubs and groups in the town.

I rang up Brighton Gay Switchboard and they told me about a social group called the Brighton Lesbian Group (BLG). I was too scared to go to any meetings but I did ask them to send me their newsletter every month. After about a year of this I decided to go to an open day they were holding at the old Resource Centre in North Road. This was in 1978. I thought I could be fairly anonymous at something like that so I went along. This event opened the door onto a whole new life for

My friend Nozzle
The wonderful thing about Nozzles is Nozzles are wonderful friends.
From Vixen

Linda Pointing

me. After that I joined the group and my confidence just rocketed. About twenty or thirty of us used to meet at the Dorset Arms every week on Wednesdays and Sundays. The landlady told her regulars we were the Ladies Sports Club.

Although BLG wasn't in itself a political organisation, it had been started by feminists. This was just about the time when feminists couldn't aspire to anything greater than being a lesbian. Although this made me angry – because I saw myself as a 'real' lesbian and these other women were just playing at it – to find a community where I was not just acceptable but positively valuable was nothing short of a miracle.

It wasn't a bed of roses, though – you didn't have an easy ride if you rubbed shoulders with feminists in those days. Everything was being questioned. All your old attitudes were turned inside out and generally found wanting. I think it is remarkable that women survived it at all. But they were determined to make changes. It was a painful process and I didn't go through it willingly. But I learnt my feminism during that time and I'd now absolutely count myself a dyed-in-the-wool feminist. I'm very grateful to those women for wrenching the scales from my eyes.

It was truly liberating to have a different way of looking at life and to not feel that you had to be apologetic about yourself – to find that you did have the courage to do things that you'd never done before. In the lesbian group, I can remember the first time we decided to have a barbecue on the beach. In order to have a barbecue on the beach you had to go to Hove Council's offices in the King Alfred and book the space. I remember going to this little room with about three or four women in their twinsets and pearls: 'And what is the group?' I took an enormous gulp and said, 'Brighton Lesbian Group', and a little hush fell upon the room. I think that was the first time I said the word 'lesbian' to someone I didn't know. That was the start of the rest of my life, really – being somebody who wasn't scared of myself. Because that's essentially what it is – if you're scared to say you're a lesbian, then you're scared of who you are.

I started working on Switchboard and got involved in the Gay Community Centre Appeal. My main contribution to that was organising the weekly fundraising disco because it was the only place for lesbians to go at the time. It started at the Hanbury Arms in Paston Place and is remembered with enormous affection by the lesbians who used to go there.

After four or five years I burnt out on doing active things. I decided to concentrate on work and my career at Brighton Planning Department. My working life was a mixture of being with very nice people, very supportive people, people who were fun to be with and a few heterosexual men who were extremely unpleasant and anti-lesbian in a polite, ironic sort of way.

In late 1987 a gay male friend at work kept coming in and putting little cuttings from various newspapers on my desk about Clause 28 that was going through parliament. It was about councils who had positive images campaigns i.e. presenting lesbians and gay men like ordinary people – not as ogres, not as mass murderers, not as child molesters but as ordinary people, with ordinary lives. The moral right thought this was terribly shocking and thought it should be stopped. It was the GLC and Haringey council who were encouraging these campaigns. I remember saying, 'Oh good God, it's only two councils, they won't have any impact on anybody. There's no point fighting against the clause because it's not going to make any difference anyway'.

Then I found out what Clause 28 actually said. It was very disturbing. It said that councils shouldn't allow schools to teach that homosexuality was acceptable as a pretended family relationship. I was alarmed that a law might be passed that called lesbians and gay men unacceptable and dismissed our relationships as not real. From then I thought, I've got to get involved in this. There were fortnightly meetings, started by a group called Brighton Lesbian Action which grew out of the Jewish Lesbian Group. I can remember writing about a thousand letters to members of the House of Lords. A lesbian friend and I sat in the library with *Burke's Peerage* and hand-wrote all the envelopes. I went to the home of some baroness in Chichester to hand deliver a letter and spoke to her on the telephone. She was quite old and had never got married so I'd decided that she might be a lesbian. I was so, so impassioned that this law should not be passed.

We weren't surprised when it was passed but I remember feeling really inspired when four dykes abseiled into the House of Lords as a protest. It was such an important gesture – it signalled our spirit of defiance. OK, you can pass your law but we're not going to take any bloody notice of it.

Sadly, Section 28 is still law. There's not much awareness of it now except in schools where it's used as an excuse to do nothing about anti-gay attitudes. I met a student teacher not long ago and she told me that she'd challenged an anti-gay remark in the classroom – like she would, routinely, with a racist remark. She'd been told by her supervisor that this contravened Section 28 and she might fail her teaching practice if she did it again. No-one's ever brought a case under Section

Linda Pointing

Meryle Philpot
For being a great role model of an adult when I was a child.
From Bunty Dann

Linda Pointing

28. It just works by people being scared of it. I really feel for young people today. It was hard enough when I was twelve or thirteen, knowing that I wasn't interested in boys and agonising over the word 'lezzie'. It wasn't a word that was used that often. Now 'gay' is a common term of abuse among young people for anything that's crap. I don't know that I'd have survived if I'd been young today.

I eventually left work in 1990 because I was very unhappy there. I thought I was going to have a breakdown if I didn't leave. So then I had even more time to devote to the things that I believed in. At about that time the campaign that had been continuing against the implementation of Section 28 changed focus and started the first Pride festivals in Brighton.

Amid all this political campaigning there were a few of us who would admit to a feeling that there was another dimension that was important but was not getting a high profile. Lesbian and Gay Spirit Rising was dedicated to symbolic actions to show our defiance. We organised a torch-lit vigil on the beach in Brighton in 1988, which was the year Section 28 became law. We stood on the beach opposite the Grand Hotel where the Tory Party conference was on. First of all we stood facing them and then we turned our backs and faced the waves – to symbolise our own strength and resilience. It was a very moving experience. I think over a hundred came. In 1990 we made giant street puppets called Hate, Fear and Ignorance and went to spook the Tories at their conference in Bournemouth.

If we're talking about achievements, my main achievement is staying the course. I'm still there, I'm still doing things, I still believe it's important. Now I look back I see things have definitely moved on but at the time you couldn't see that you were having much of an impact at all. You had to believe that your drop in the ocean, along with everybody else's drop in the ocean makes quite a lot of water and it *does* make waves.

One of the other things that I've been involved with is the Brighton Ourstory Project, lesbian and gay history group. For the last ten years we've been unearthing lesbians and gay men who would tell us their life stories. We tried to aim for people who were older than us. We wanted to know what it was like living in a time when male homosexuality was against the law. People had the most amazing array of strategies and weapons to help them survive in a world that basically did not want them to exist and they told us all about them – as well as about the funny and romantic times.

The Trades Council were wanting to do a book about ordinary folk in Brighton and they asked us to do a chapter. So

Linda Pointing

we started interviewing and discovered that Brighton for a long, long time had been a real centre for lesbians and gay men and was particularly vibrant in the fifties and sixties. We were doing quite well when we learnt that the Trades Council had dropped the project so we decided we could do our own book about that era.

We published *Daring Hearts* in 1992 with Queen Spark Books. Before that we had done a show called Really Living, which was a kind of generation by generation skate through the last 150 years of Brighton's lesbian and gay history. Composer and pianist, Michael Finnessy got us a Brighton Festival event and we did quite an elaborate production with him composing and playing the piano. We had video images and actors reading the words of the individuals that we had interviewed. It went down a storm and it started a tradition of the Brighton Ourstory Project putting on shows and exhibitions at the Brighton Festival.

Another tradition that's continued for ten years is laying a pink triangle wreath at the war memorial on Remembrance Day. We realised that there were loads of lesbians and gay men who were deeply in the closet but nevertheless had done their bit and we wanted to acknowledge their contribution. The organisers of the ceremony and the police were very resistant to us to start with and for years we were prevented from laying our wreath at the same time as everyone else – although we did try. Happily now there's been a change of heart and in 1998 we were an official part of the ceremony for the first time. Also for the first time ever they didn't announce who any of the wreath-layers were. I don't know if they realise how insulting that was.

Anyway, it's been a very moving experience to have done it because when we weren't allowed to lay the wreath until all the dignitaries had gone, lots of people came up and read the inscription while we were standing there. I actually had to read it out to one old lady in a woolly hat and I was waiting – waiting to get a mouthful of abuse from her because the words 'homosexual', 'gay', 'lesbian' appear throughout – but she said, "Thank-you, dear," and that just made it all worthwhile.

Emma Rigby
My wonderful daughter.
From Sue Rigby

Liz Williams

Liz came to Brighton from Gloucestershire to do a Masters Degree in Philosophy in 1987.

In the autumn of 1995 I met Rosemary Lovatt, who was then the secretary of the Women's Centre and I wanted to get involved with something because I was doing a lot of work in the commercial sector. Basically I had an idea that I wanted to get more involved in voluntary projects, I wanted to get involved in women's projects, and I wanted to do something a bit less mercenary if you like, and give something back, and also Rosemary seemed extremely sane, which was kind of a prerequisite because I had a high lunatic meter running! The Management Committee of the Brighton Women's Centre always seemed to be extremely stable and very sensible. She encouraged me to come along and I worked on rota until the summer of 1998.

I write science fiction. I've always been a science fiction fan, not just the sort of Star Trek stuff on TV. My mother started writing gothic horror when I was a child and she had about twelve books published. She wrote sort of gothic romances and then when I was about twelve or thirteen she started getting into science fiction as well. I thought, wow, this is a whole different world. I wasn't particularly enamoured with the world that I was in, I wanted to be somewhere else, I always wanted to travel and this was an easy way to do it when you're twelve years old. Shortly after that I started reading a lot of the feminist writing and the 70s was a big time for feminist science fiction – people like Susy McKee Charnas and Ursula LeGuin – who wrote the kind of anthropological literature which explored society and gender, rather than 'shoot ups' in space, which were very much the boys' stuff.

When I finished my doctorate, I felt that I'd had enough of academic writing, and I wanted to try some fiction. I started writing short stories, and a couple of novels. The short stories have been published, the novels haven't – the usual story! It [science fiction] seems a 'blokey' thing – I mean by that a 'nerdy' thing. It still has a connotation of little boys in anoraks watching Star Trek and there's a lot more to it than that. It's a good forum for exploring gender issues, and there is some very good feminist science fiction around at the moment. I think that needs to be encouraged – there certainly seems to be a little nexus of SF in Brighton. For some unknown reason it just seems to have gravitated down here.

I am in the Co-ordinating Committee [of Brighton Women's Centre], and I've also been involved in *Broadsheet*. I'm committed to the Centre for pragmatic reasons rather than ideological reasons. As far as a 'women-only space' is concerned, if it's pouring with rain and there's a bloke standing outside the door and his girlfriend's in for a pregnancy test, I'll let him in. I'm not particularly into the idea of women-only space for myself, it doesn't really matter to me. But it does matter to others, like our clients, and that's why I think it needs to be preserved and encouraged, because it is there for them.

The Women's Centre certainly needs to expand, this is the big problem, and at the moment we're in the process of going round looking at properties, and trying to get grants, which is a real chicken and egg situation – do we apply for the money first? Or do we find a suitable building and then apply for the money? But we're making a serious effort to move now because it's just getting ridiculous. The Women's Centre will move, because we have to, and I think it will expand. It will have to change to a large degree because of the nature of the funding we're receiving; whenever you get funding they [the funders] want a hierarchy. The Unemployment Centre has found this, and we've found this. If we did get another large grant we will have to install a hierarchy, and we're going to resist this like mad. They need patriarchy, to use the old fashioned phrase – they need structure, they need hierarchy. So we're going to have to play along, if we want to grow. And that I think is going to be an interesting question to consider in the future.

It [the Women's Centre] has certainly given another dimension to my life. I came out of academia and I worked in the commercial world for quite a long time, and [the voluntary sector] just is a whole different way of thinking, and a whole different approach to hierarchical versus flat structures. I think it's politically very interesting in terms not necessarily of what we achieve but what we try to achieve. There's always going to be a gap between aims and objectives and actual practice, and there are always going to be problems with things that have tried to be democratically run because there comes a point in which someone digs their heels and says, no, 'you're going to go my way'. And that's the problem you get with all democracies. I've always been a feminist and I'm not one of those people who says, 'Oh well, of course all that's old hat, all that's over now' – it's not over. There is still a political need for equality, in terms of the political and the professional arenas. And I don't believe in post-feminism. I tend to turn round to women who say, 'Well, of course I've never been a feminist', and I say, 'Well, you're standing here in your high heels with your good job, and come next May you're going to go out and vote, what do you mean you're not a feminist? This is what your Grandmothers tied themselves to the railings for'. Sexism very definitely isn't dead.

Liz Williams

Rachel Pinney
– who died in 1995 at the age of 86. She was one of the first female doctors in the UK, she was a committed member of the CND and for 30 years kept silent on Wednesdays as a protest against nuclear weapons. She pioneered child therapeutic techniques such as 'Creative Listening' and Children's Hours, which are now widely used by experts around the world and yet she was largely ignored by the therapeutic community. Rachel you were a pure genius, unorthodox, eccentric, principled, funny and honest – I hope the world won't forget you.
From Kelle Kingsley

Michelle Pooley

"I lived in Wales and had been involved in running the Swansea Women's Centre in a voluntary capacity and learnt the ropes of working in the voluntary sector through my work with women's organisations: Women's Aid, Women's Refuges, CAB's, Women's groups at the universities. I worked both for some of them and with them.

I've been the Co-ordinator at Brighton Women's Centre for two-and-a-half years now. I think it's a great organisation. The principles and objectives of working with women, especially women on low incomes, trying to work with them for their own self-esteem, trying to empower them, is fundamental to what a women's centre should be about. I think the personalities of the people, the environment that it's in is great, but I think it's now got to the stage where the space that it's in is just amazingly small. I think that any organisation that has multi-talented people, multi-grade attitudes, it's always going to be a difficult task. Coming into a completely voluntary agency with one worker, to being somebody who's supposed to be co-ordinating the Centre is going to be a rocky ride. But I've enjoyed it, it's going to be challenging.

Michelle Pooley

For the first year in my job, I spent the first six months making sure that I knew what the organisation was about, understanding exactly how the systems worked, networking with outside agencies making sure that they knew about us. The next six months was trying to put in systems of evaluation, monitoring, getting right to the crux of how the services work and trying to make them better. The following was marred by very difficult circumstances, both personal for myself, and also about the things that were going on in the Centre. But now we're at the stage where we've had a development day, we've got the business plan to a point where we can start thinking about marketing. This year (1999), is solely about making working groups work, getting funding, pulling us together as a team. And about looking at what we really want to be doing.

In the early 1990s I was a student who had decided to do Computer Science at university. I did do a year of Geology, but decided that as a woman, it wouldn't be very appropriate for me to go and sit on an oil-rig for ten months, in a very male-orientated world. So I swapped to Computer Science, thinking that I could go and do a Geology Masters afterwards. But I was in a classroom of sixty men, started off with four female colleagues which went down to two. I went in search for something other than computer screens. I ended up as a Student Union officer, although I actually first went in there just to try and find female friends.

I worked my way through college with no funding at all. In the student bar, and cleaning out the minibuses for £10 a week, all the dirt and the vomit! And I got involved in women's politics because of issues around childcare and safety.

We were quite radical, in those days, doing student protests. We ensured we had active participation by the university trying to improve the childcare on the campus. I was very active in the Women's Group, which worked on issues of the day that were relevant to women students. In the case of some issues e.g. childcare, we felt that women should be able to decide what action they wanted to take in a women-only environment, but if men wanted to join in they could, once the decisions had been made. It wasn't for them to be in the Women's Group making the decisions. We were as a group really clear on this. That worked really well. In fact, we managed to get a sabbatical post as a women's officer in Swansea university. I started up a night-line, and then I went on into research.

I found it really difficult that when student sabbatical officers were standing it was always on party political lines. It had always been my ethos that students were fighting for the needs

Julia Reddaway
Julia's ability to listen, combined with a practical nature, concise knowledge and boundless enthusiasm, has ensured that those of us who are lucky enough to know her, are constantly filled with a sense of wonder and gratitude.
From Marcelle Bruzas

Michelle Pooley

of students, that no political party would ever fulfill all of our needs and wants. So I stood just as a woman, coming from a science background, and got amazing support from the men in my year, got elected and carried on. So when I stood for NUS Wales sabbaticals, I stood on a non-party political ticket and got in.

I did a lot of work, with the Equal Opportunities Commission, with FairPlay, a children's organisation, with the Aids Network Trust across Wales. I did training with Women's Officers, made sure that Women's Officers in all the colleges knew what they were doing, held rallies and all sorts of mad student things.

I would very definitely define myself as a feminist. I just believe that feminism is about equality for women, as well as for men. Like if you go for a job there should be equality in terms of pay for the job you're doing, not in terms of your gender. Some people see me as a radical feminist, but I would say that I am an international feminist. I believe in solidarity, in collective working. I don't believe in patriarchy. I don't think it has any place in life. I do believe in matriarchy. There are a lot of good things about women, the way we work, how we can work collectively, how we can also be very honest sometimes.

There's always a place for feminism, but I think that over the years it has had a kind of dirty label attached to it which I don't agree with. We've had the whole rise of a new feminism, which is resultant from people like the Spice Girls which has had a really good effect for young women. But I just wonder what women really think of as feminism. It's now labelled as 'girl-power', which really annoys me, I mean you don't go out and say 'boy-power', that turns into man-power. I think 'girl-power' is great for youngsters, and then once you get to 16, 17, 18 you begin to start realising that you're actually a woman.

I think feminism will always have a place in society. I think most women are feminists, they might not label themselves as such, but they believe in equality. What worries me is that women will actually overtake men and be more powerful than them. I wouldn't want to live in a world that's like that. Young boys are underachieving and girls are achieving very good grades, and I think we have to look at the ways that boys and girls are taught. But as a feminist I do believe that boys are the product of both male and female, and that women do have to make sure that boys have to understand that it's ok to be a boy who likes to sew, that's just what your gifts are. Just as if girls want to play rugby, or go abseiling.

Michelle Pooley

The most amazing thing is that a small group of women grew into an organisation that is now as big as this. And how 25 years on I will walk round Brighton and people will say, 'I was there 25 years ago', or 'seventeen years ago'. I don't think it's been an easy metamorphosis of women working together. There've always been issues where after discussion women have not seen eye-to-eye on certain issues. But what I do think is wonderful about it, is it was voluntary for almost 20 years. So many women have got so much out of it.

Diane Smith
For climbing the mountain.
From Kelle Kingsley

Molly Wadey

Molly has lived in Brighton all her life. She was born in the Richmond Street area, and talks about her working life and family.

"I returned to working for BT in 1978, I worked for them first of all in the 60s, between my children and then I got pregnant with my eldest son and I didn't go back to them again until '78 and I worked as a telephonist in Brighton. I heard that they were requiring some engineers on the private wire duty and I had a word with one or two of the lads and they told me who I had to reply to. I thought that at my age I'd have no chance, but I was lucky. I was 47 then. I joined the group, at first it was a bit of a big joke for these boys, as they were all much younger than me, I was the only woman. I had to be one of lads, do everything they did and then be accepted. So that is what I did. I started going out with and helping each one of them and in the end I was just one of the lads. There was an eight-month training period. At college I was accepted just the same and I got my overhead training and passed on that. The job was called a OMI – a one man installer, and I used to say I'm a OPI – a one person installer!

Molly Wadey

Then I went out on my own. I loved my job so much I would have gone to work for nothing! That was exactly how much I loved it, climbing poles, doing the heavy work, drilling walls was all part of it. The beauty of this job was, with the specific group that I was with, you sort of did the whole thing.

One of the most enjoyable things that comes to mind, was when the Big Breakfast Show came to Brighton on the sea front – I get tingles thinking of it. I was involved in installing the line there and they had it on the side of the pier on the groyne and they said 'Molly would you like to be the onsite engineer for the Big Breakfast?' just in case anything went down I could have a look and get in touch with anybody else if necessary and see what was going on. I went back in the morning, it was a lovely sunny morning and all the crowds were there and I went through with my little case and the thing that affected me was that as the sun came up you see all these youngsters – the stage was on the groyne facing westwards and as far as you could see there were these faces and I just stood there watching these youngsters thoroughly enjoying themselves. The sun was coming up and it was a lovely, lovely atmosphere and I think that I will always remember that day.

In 1996, I was then coming up 55, there was early voluntary retirement if you wanted it and I thought, you can't be Peter Pan forever, I've done it, I've enjoyed it and it's time to make way for the young people now and I decided to go for early voluntary retirement. At first it was really, really strange, like a fish out of water, my sister-in-law still worked at the exchange so I still used to hear a few things, how were the lads, whether they'd had babies or got married or someone else had retired. In the January after I had retired, by word of mouth I heard that they were wanting contract engineers, not to work directly for BT. I applied to a few of the agencies and I became involved in the change over of the equipment of a few of the exchanges in the area, so really I went back to them. It wasn't really until April '98 that I have not had work, and I also have my first grandchild, who was born two days later.

I have lived in Brighton all my life. I was born in the Richmond Street area, which is no longer there. A lot of it was bombed in the war and they have re-built it now and that's where I was born. I went to St John's Junior and then on to Elm Grove Girls School. When I was young the North Laines were just like for ordinary people, most of them rented their homes, everyone rented their homes in those days. When we were children we really didn't take much notice of the Lanes and the Royal Pavilion was about the

My Daughter Alison
(June 1964 to May 1969).
She didn't have the opportunities in this life.
From Molly Wadey

Molly Wadey

most we took interest in and we used to go over to the museum after school as it was just down the road from school.

We would all go to the Regent on Saturday night, which was lovely, and we could wander down to the bottom, walk home, us girls all together and we'd all meet up with other people walking home and you'd need not worry about anything at all, you were safe. There wasn't the violence. My predominate time was the late 50s, I was married at 19. You had the extreme ones who dressed as Teddy boys but then you had the ones in like the Italian suits then, I never really saw any violence, they talked of cut throat razors and things like that but not in Brighton.

My first child was a little girl, we lost her to meningitis very, very suddenly over three days in 1969. I had also at that time had a little boy who was 18 months old. I had the boy and the girl, the pigeon pair. You never get over it, and then I had another little boy a year later. So I went from having a little girl and everything being girlie for four, nearly five years to completely the other way, to all boys. You learn to live with it, some days it's as if it was yesterday, that's why Florence is so special, my granddaughter, she's beautiful.

It's nice to think that women can sort of think, 'I'd like to do that' and be allowed to do it and be capable of doing it and be encouraged to do it if they want to do it. We've had a lady PM, I think that if we are capable of doing the job then hopefully we will be accepted, it will be a fact of life.

Nic Fryer

Brighton was my favourite town because of holidays and day trips to the seaside so when I went to university I chose Sussex. The university found you somewhere to live, which was great, it was a guest house right on the seafront, opposite the West Pier.

That's when I met the women's movement. The woman in the room next door was from women's liberation. She talked about it a lot and some of us got interested. I started going to Women's Liberation General meetings in 1971. I sat there for a good two or three years without opening my mouth. It was very scary. The women there were more grown-up than me. Decision-making was based on consensus – and lots of arguments. There were national conferences in those days, too – lots of building up of national organisations like National Abortion Campaign, National Women's Aid. There was a strong network, nationwide. All the major towns had their own women's liberation groups and newsletters.

It was all just starting and growing at exactly the same time I was. It was like my whole life made sense for the first time ever. Through reading and talking to other women you found out that other women's experience was similar to your own and that what you thought was a personal problem was something that happened to everybody. You could look at it politically and analyse what was going on.

The biggest controversies were between the socialists and the radical feminists. The socialist women would say, 'You lot aren't political, you must join our political party,' and we'd say, 'Your political party does nothing for women. We're the real voice of women'. There was a move towards separatism. We were going to be the ones who started the revolution. First we'd all refuse to get married. It was about putting women first and making a political analysis of the world starting from yourself, which is where personal politics comes from. We knew that if women moved the whole world would move because we were at the bottom of it all. I still believe that.

We were doing all this political stuff together. There was the campaign to start a women's centre, the abortion campaign, setting up a women's refuge in the town. So it meant I spent a lot of time in the evenings at meetings with women but there was no really social time with them. So one of the other exciting things that happened was women-only social events. We started to have a social life together without men, which

To all my girl friends
– who have been an inspiration, in one way or another, in my life.
From Jackie Cairns

Nic Fryer

was seen as very, very threatening to everybody's boyfriends and husbands. I still had a boyfriend who I saw every weekend while I was at university. I don't know what he felt about me going to women-only socials but the first one I went to was when I first had sex with a woman. I got very drunk and stayed after everyone else had gone home and had a nice time on this woman's living room floor with the woman who had been my best friend in politics.

A lot of us were living together but nobody was lesbian – as far as we knew. The word hadn't crept in yet. A couple of women moved down to Brighton who were quite dynamic and quite obviously lesbians – nobody could invisible-ise them – and the Women's Liberation General Meetings got barred from the Prince George pub in Trafalgar Street because they held hands in there. We moved to the Catholic Chaplaincy, believe it or not – part of Sussex University. That's where we had the historic meeting where the word 'lesbian' was first ever mentioned at a Brighton Women's Liberation General Meeting. We were discussing this incident of getting chucked out of this pub. The best bit of the entire argument – that probably swayed it in the direction of supporting lesbians – was our resident intellectual said, 'If we give carte blanche support to lesbians, next they'll be buggering cats'. At which everyone was a bit shocked. So we decided we would give support to lesbians and make that a visible part of the women's movement.

After that there was no holding it back. Those of us that had been walking around, holding hands and generally spending every waking minute together suddenly thought, ooh-er perhaps that's what we are. I thought, that's what I definitely am. This particular woman that I'd made love with at the party definitely wasn't.

Then I fell in love with a woman who was a lesbian and she loved me back and it was wonderful. She said, 'My advice to you is, don't go out with women who aren't lesbians,' and it's the best advice I've ever been given. Along with all the other wonderful things that were happening in my life it was the most wonderful. Lots and lots of lovely sex with lovely women, that I was doing important things with, that were going to change the world.

The Women's Centre opened in November 1974. It was in Buckingham Road. We got this huge building that Social Services passed on to us. We tarted it up a bit and thought of functions for all the rooms. There were rows in the Women's Centre collective over lesbians being out there. Some women said, 'It's off-putting to the woman in the street'. We said, 'The woman in the street might be a lesbian too'.

Nic Fryer

That same year we started having women-only discos. We got a tape deck and had tapes of women's music. Women lent money to buy the equipment and then got it back as money was raised on the door. There were big rows. Should it be all women's music? Should it be only women vocalists? We did discos at the university, rooms above pubs in town, women's private parties.

Then a woman arrived on the scene who said, 'Let's get serious about this disco business. Let's do it with records'. I liked being a DJ. I was always a bit too embarrassed to dance, so behind the deck was much the favourite place for me to be. You have to be a bit bossy to be a DJ and keeping them dancing is quite a challenge. I was part of a collective at first so I didn't always get to be the one who put the music on. We had to take it in turns lifting the equipment and shifting it. Every venue was either upstairs or downstairs.

I started working at Sussex University Student Union shop and did the Gaysoc discos for many years. They were the most popular discos on campus. Apparently a lot of women who saw me around thought, oooh, there's a lesbian.

Non-political lesbians used to come to our discos in town. We thought, they'll walk in through that door and we'll convert them all to feminism and they were laughing up their sleeves at us. 'These girls,' they called us. They called us all sorts of names. There was a friendly rivalry between the two groups.

In 1979 three of us started doing Disco Dykes Extravaganzas on Friday nights at the Silver Slipper Club, which was through Waitrose car park and up some stairs. It was almost unheard of then for women to be DJs. All the club DJs were men. People thought women couldn't do it. It was women only in the dancing part. There were some embarrassing moments for the women who were doing the door who couldn't tell that some of the bar dykes were women.

Soon after that we went on to the Hanbury Arms. We did alternate weeks with the bloke who was the DJ for Dymples Gay Disco on Friday nights. That was very successful and very big for several years. It was really good there – up on a podium, a bit more scary. It was a fundraiser for the Gay Centre Fund. For me, it didn't really matter that the money was going towards a gay centre, it was the fact of having the discos that was important.

At one of our venues in Kemp Town the landlord used to hang around with his men friends and let them watch the lesbians dancing together. We always hated it and we used to argue with him and say, 'Look, we're paying for this room,

Rosemary Creighton-Sessions
My mother, who gave the best of her heart in the name of love. Thank you.
From Jenny Sessions

Nic Fryer

keep your bloody friends upstairs'. And he didn't and the end result was a nasty fight. Two women badly beaten up by several of these men. So that was it, we never went back there.

We went to the basement of the Palace Pier Hotel on the seafront. That was quite a laugh – it had been a gay men's club for years so I felt like an intruder and I think quite a lot of feminist women did. When that hotel went bust in the mid-eighties, we moved to the basement of the Churchill Palace Hotel in Middle Street. It was predominantly women and it was all women DJ-ing by then so some of us wanted to make it a women-only disco officially and stop having boys there at all. We got quite a lot of telling off from the non-feminist women saying, 'You man-haters, what's wrong with them?' But in the end they came round because there wasn't much else to.

By then the emphasis for me, definitely had gone away from that being a feminist activity to being something that I did because it had to be done. You couldn't disappoint all those women who were relying on you. It was still fun and it was still the basis of my social life but it was no longer, 'I'm going to change the world by doing these discos'. It was, 'Well, this is what life's about – you've got to have somewhere to go on a Friday night'. In the end I just helped a lot of lesbians to meet each other.

Norma Binnie

Norma first came to Brighton in 1970 from London, a long route from Teeside starting as a runaway at sixteen, ending up in London, one marriage, one divorce then packed herself off to Art School. She ran off with her tutor, finally married him, came down to Brighton from Earl's Court, leaving everything behind because her ex-husband was pursuing her. This year Norma was awarded an honorary degree from Sussex University as a recognition for her work in the arts.

We thought there was no fit place to live between London and the coast and in those days, 1970, you couldn't get a flat in Earl's Court for love nor money and when we came to Brighton we flogged round agents and got a bit tired. My partner said, 'let's knock on the door of an old actor friend of mine', but he didn't know where he lived, but being an artist he was visually trained and he thought, architecturally I'll know exactly where he is. And that was absolutely true and we turned up at First Avenue, Hove and there on the first house from the sea was this sign, Two Bedroom Flat to Let, to include heating, unfurnished. We

Shirley Smith
Shirley was not only a great sister but also my best friend. We experienced evacuation during the war and later saw our hours demolished during the London blitz, but we had each other for support. We also had great fun together during our teens!
From Mimi Blackwell

Norma Binnie

couldn't believe it, it was like a joke. So we went and knocked on the door and this little old lady in a hairnet and pink nylon overall and fluffy slippers came out and she was the caretaker and we said we're interested in the flat. And she said, 'Are you students?', we umm'd and aahh'd a bit, then one of us said, yes, and the other said, no! And she took us in this rickety lift to the second floor and as we were going up in this lift, she said, 'Are you married?' and again we stumbled over this one and then said, 'yes' then there was a pause and he said, 'but not to each other.' She opened the door and there was this amazing flat, we felt like Citizen Kane… we couldn't believe our luck. She said they wanted £16 a week for it and this was a great blow because this was an enormous amount of money. We had to go and sit on the beach and throw endless pebbles in the sea and decide…

So that was our introduction to Brighton and Hove. We got very 'in love' with Hove as opposed to Brighton because of where we lived, we got very involved and worried about the elderly population. There were some terribly interesting people, one in particular called Bijou O'Connor. When we met her she was well into her seventies with only one leg. The other one was a wooden one she screwed in each day. She came from aristocracy and she'd drag this poor Pekinese behind her, called Ming, and lived in an absolute hovel. Why we adored Bijou was probably for all the wrong reasons, she was an out-and-out fascist, she'd got to the age where she could say the most outrageous things and comments… but you can only get away with it if you have an eccentricity because it draws people to you. I think it's good to aspire to rapidly ageing juvenile delinquency! Yet she was somebody who had had money and she represented a whole cross-section of people at that time, living in bedsits in wonderful mansion houses. But what went on behind the doors was another story, absolute poverty. They were proud people and wouldn't ask for any help no matter how many times you told them what their rights were, so we decided that we had to look after them, which we did very quietly. It culminated in an exhibition that we called, 'The Spirit of Hove' and it wasn't a particularly joyous exhibition… I had built a replica of Bijou's bedsit, complete with smell and all memories… the exhibition was at Hove Museum and within one day of it opening, the Council, led by the leader of the Council, came to close it down; this was not Hove at all! It culminated in it being on television and the Museum was forced to keep it on as a slice of what was really going on in this town… I don't know that it made a great difference, but I do think the power of art is enormous and I've

Norma Binnie

remained a campaigner in whatever way. That introduced us to one aspect of living in this town where it was the old people who were being discriminated against.

I come from a school of thought and conditioning, to grow up, not get qualifications, hopefully meet someone who had a clerical job and keep me for the rest of my life. Very early on I knew that I didn't want that, but I didn't see that I had to get equality with males, I just assumed that I was equal and I've always assumed that, so in a way I've never suffered from being made to feel different because I was a woman. I haven't suffered from any blatant sexual discrimination or maybe it's been there and I haven't noticed it because I've been too arrogant to notice it. On each step of my career ladder, it's been a man who has encouraged me, so in a way it's been the reverse of any discrimination. Maybe that's because I've been in the art world, which like most worlds has been dominated by men and it's only really in the last 40 years that female artists are seen in the history of art books. At college all the tutors were men and the first person to encourage me was my tutor, who ended up being my husband. As we're talking something is crystallising here because we were both artists, but I bowed out of producing my own art, even after this controversial and successful exhibition at Hove Museum. It was a bit like, 'there's only room for one artist in the household', and I think I did make that conscious decision, 'and if so, he is the better one'. I made that decision and so I went into the administration side, encouraged, of course, by the practising artist.

We were very selfish really looking back… you don't really think of other people at the time of passion, it's only you that matters… The rules were that if we got together then we were travelling light, with no children and I, of course, went along with that, so madly, deeply lovingly accepting, and so I went on the pill. I had never been on the pill before, and of course what happened ten years later, I got pregnant. I was absolutely beside myself with guilt, that was the overriding feeling and I didn't know I was pregnant until I was three and a half months because it was the last thing I, or my doctor, were looking for. I felt like I'd let him down, that I'd broken the rules, this wasn't meant to happen and my doctor was urging me to make a decision. Immediately when she told me I said, 'I can't have it, I'd agreed not to.' My husband was away in France and I had to wait until he got back and I blurted it out in tears and I remember he didn't look at me, he just paced the room with his hands behind his back and said, 'Well you know what we agreed'. So the next day I went to Wiston's abortion clinic on

Maria Margaret Puffett
She was a wonderful mother.
From Maude Blackwell

Norma Binnie

Dyke Road. They insisted on me seeing a counsellor and doctor, I couldn't speak to either of them coherently because of crying. I couldn't see any real reason for giving up this baby, I was in a stable relationship with no particular money worries, but I had broken the rules… I knew also, at age 36, being pregnant for the first time, that I wouldn't have another chance and if I went ahead with the abortion, I felt that I didn't deserve another chance either. Anyway, I did go through it and I paid the £70 in advance. There was a young girl in the bed opposite me and this was her third time there and I felt such revulsion, she was happy about being there and I was convulsed in tears. It was probably the worse experience of my life. My doctor told me that if I didn't put it behind me, it would probably wreck my life, but it did wreck the relationship which went on for 20 years. My husband's son very sadly committed suicide about six months later and I think this is about the cruellest thing that has ever been said to me, he said, 'If only you hadn't had that abortion.' It's like when iron enters the soul then, on a moment like that, especially when he had refused to have a vasectomy. I thought, how dare you still be able to procreate as you more or less forced me to kill our child and now your child has killed himself and you're turning it round like it's my fault. So that was a very very bad period for me personally and I couldn't share it with anybody because I felt so ashamed at what I'd done. I never admitted to anybody until about ten or twelve years later, I couldn't even think about it without crying. I don't particularly have any views about termination today, I certainly wouldn't advise anybody one way or the other, I'm just very pleased that the choice is there.

It changed my life quite dramatically. Especially the next morning my husband bought me a puppy and I'm afraid it wasn't sufficient compensation but over the years the dogs have become the children and my dog today is my baby, I make no apologies for that.

In 1986 I had to give up working in London because I developed cervical cancer which had gone sufficiently far that it needed an operation and I really felt that commuting was too much for me. I found a local job with a PR company, which was a one-man band and me. Although I was quite skilled in office procedures I hadn't bashed a typewriter for years. On the first day I could see the owner's face at the errors I was making. At that time I was a nail biter, so I had false nails on and hadn't taken account of typing with them and within hours they kept pinging off and hitting the wrong keys. Just another saga in wearing false things as I have done in my

Mimi Blackwell
My mum, the angel with the chubby legs who has always been on my side. Thank you.
From Jackie Blackwell

Norma Binnie

youth, leaving false eyelashes on blokes' cheeks and stockings coming out of my bra… here I was thirty years later still being seduced by false things! However, I never behaved as if I was the lackey, I behaved as though I was the partner! And one day I saw a job at the Gardner Arts Centre for an administrator and I thought that was absolutely perfect… and I did get the job. My illness was put behind me and I was 42 when I took the job and full of energy, life and this was a new chapter in my life. I was also very fortunate to meet someone else who was to become my third husband and we are great soul mates and passionately in love!

It was a wrench to leave the Gardner Arts Centre after ten years, but it was a right decision of mine because the achievements over the ten years were greater than the disappointments so therefore, that was the right time to go. I felt I had achieved my ambitions I had there so my time was worthwhile. And now the next phase of my life will no doubt be very different and I really don't know what's going to unfold. I'm sure it will be interesting whatever it is.

The many faces of Norma Binnie – from her graduation show in the 60s

Chris Abuk
– a warm and wonderful person who has been an inspiration for many, many women. I'm so glad that we met and became friends.
From Jackie Blackwell

Pat

"I come from quite a right-wing reactionary background but in '79 after I had my second child, I saw a crèche advertised in town and it was for a woman's study course. It wasn't run by the Women's Centre, it was run by the WEA. I went on it and it was the most wonderful thing. It was two days a week and it was free, it was about 15 women, we came from very different educational backgrounds, some women couldn't read, so women were doing different levels of education. Through the course I got involved with women's politics. A couple of the women on the course were involved in the Brighton Women's Centre, so I went along to try it, which was then at the Brighthelm Centre. I think I hung around outside for months, I was petrified. I was still very conservative – I felt like I was very prim looking. I was petrified because these women, who were coming out, seemed so full of themselves. I don't mean that in a negative way, I mean that they were confident and strong and I felt like such a drip and I hung around for months. I used to go backwards and forwards and in the end I came up with the idea that I'd go in and ask about my sister's menopause! So I went and I thought, this is wonderful, and I actually said to the woman who was so lovely, that I had been frightened to come in. I began to go to meetings, there were huge meetings and there were, what seemed to me, hundreds of women. It was when there was the first abortion bill, about that time, and then there were little sub-groups started from that. You went to people's houses to discuss different issues and at that time I hardly joined in because I felt I didn't have a clue what was going on, educationally.

In the early 80s, the Women's Centre was above the vegetarian food shop in George Street. You used to have to go through the shop. An older woman's group got set up through that, which I was involved with, because I was an older woman, even then, it was about 1980. Then of course Greenham began, which was wonderful and I was going to Greenham between '83 and '86. There was a women's camp set up on the Level here, where they pitched tents and they set up for about six or seven months as a protest camp. I think they got moved on in the end.

I also joined a consciousness-raising group in about 1980 and that was very hot, oh it was hot. You had to be very careful that you were 'sisterly' enough with each other. It felt like they

Pat

could shout at you, but you couldn't shout at anybody else. I found that quite difficult. It was very sociologically based – consciousness-raising – whereas I come from a psychology background.

Then the Centre moved to this one at Lettice House. I remember it just being rubble, I remember digging out rubble, getting down under the floorboards and tipping out all this rubble, it was really hard going and the loo used to flood!

I used to pretend I wasn't married and for years I thought I couldn't possibly be a feminist because I wasn't radical enough, because I lived with a man! Even though people didn't know that I lived with a man, just the fact that I lived with a man meant that I wasn't politically correct and my consciousness wasn't raised enough. It felt as if there was a group that set the theory and everyone had to fit in and because I hadn't got any background in political thinking I thought I had to follow that, whereas if I came into it now I would say, 'hold on I don't agree', but then I didn't.

You hear people saying 'I'm not one of those feminists' and I hate it because it's got nothing to do with the reality, it's a stereotype. Somebody said the other day about bra burning, there was never a bra burnt, where has this myth come from!

I am terribly involved with women's issues in my own way. I am constantly sticking up for women, I'm doing my own consciousness-raising in terms of correcting people about what I think is bad behaviour from men, and correcting stereotypes. I think that I have actually grown up through other women. I was brought up in children's homes by nuns, so I had a very oppressive upbringing by other women, but I needed to work it through with women.

In ten years' time I might be retired and will probably get involved with the Women's Centre again, I'd like to join an older women's group. I don't think that I need one at the moment. I never feel as though I've left the Centre, it's just that I'm not daily involved, I just breeze in and breeze out.

Erica Smith
– saviour in our hour of need. Thank you.
From Women's Words

Polly Marshall

Polly spent her childhood in London in the swinging sixties, the Sussex countryside in the Seventies, moved to Bexhill when she was at school, came to Brighton for a weekend in 1985 and decided to stay.

"I was Chair of Brighton Women's Environmental Network and I gave it up to do an MA in contemporary literature. I originally studied at Oxford but they're pretty old fashioned, so I decided to catch up on the 20th century and as part of my MA I was writing about how society deals with ecological issues and apocalypse, mutation, that sort of thing. I read a book called *Watchmen* by Alan Moore, and he was kind enough to let me interview him for my paper. At the end of the evening he said, 'If you want to organise an event in Brighton I can do it'. So when I finished my MA I thought what do I do? There wasn't much happening, so I booked Alan and he did a reading and it was really successful. That was in 1993 and now we've won awards and had more fun than you can shake a stick at generally!

We [Do Tongues] promote contemporary literature and give authors exhibition space for their work. There are certain authors

Polly Marshall

who are really keen on the performance side of their work, so they will tour and read, or there are some poets who are very involved in the performance side, so for those kinds of people we put on different events. We've been in many places, we never stay anywhere – nobody owns us, like a pirate ship that goes from one island to another and picks up what it wants.

I haven't really had any criticism [about Do Tongues] but I think there have been times when it's been very difficult running a business and having to be tough about things to survive and sometimes people don't like that. So I kind of made a conscious decision to work with women really – I love men, I adore them and we've got lots of men who help with things, but when it comes to working with people on a non-stop basis, I really feel that I have to work with women.

I worked a lot with Kathy Acker before she died that was interesting, very special. I liked her, she was a real career woman. She loved coming down to Brighton, she used to make me go and see flats with her all the time. She was thinking about moving down here, but she got stuck in London instead. So that was an extraordinary partnership and I was privileged to be a friend of Kath's. It was very sad for me personally when she died, but it was interesting to see what the papers ran, two days after Kathy died, because of they way she was. Because she was counter-culture, pierced, proud and magnificent and outspoken with it, the 'cardigan wearing' brigade in the Guardian were criticising her and I thought that was amazing that they could be so rude and thoughtless. But Kathy was an amazing woman. She did a reading at Do Tongues, October 1996, wearing a see-through shirt when she'd just had her double mastectomy – it was really awesome.

My latest thing is writing this play with Fireraisers about a Brighton woman Phoebe Hessel. She lived to 108 and fought as a soldier in the Napoleonic Wars. It's been great working on my own writing, quite a challenge and really hard work but I love it. Working in theatre is really interesting, a cross between written and spoken word. Phoebe's premier is in Taking Liberties this year and we have an older actress playing Old Phoebe and a woman director so it's a real all-girl original. And a strong woman story is very interesting to write, I think there should be more of them and less of the victim stuff.

It was a right eye-opener researching working women's history because there is naff all about working class women in the Eighteenth Century so I drew a lot on folk ballads and my imagination. All the information I had about Phoebe was from her oral history, just like this, interviews she had given in Brighton when she was more than a 100 years old. So although

Inge
For all the endless words of wisdom, love and encouragement.
From Sue McFarlane

Polly Marshall

it's a true story, she often contradicts herself and I love that gossipy element, it brings history to life.

When I look at young women and how confident they can be, I think, yes girl, go for it, don't let anything hold you back. I think it's a self esteem thing, build your self esteem, believe in what you're doing. You can't change things without going out there and doing it. It took me a long time to find something that I really, really liked doing and to let myself do that and I think that's very difficult and a lot of women lack confidence. So it's a kind of economy of confidence and economy generally; women always end up being worse paid than blokes because anything that we do is somehow undervalued. A woman's work is never done, it's never paid for either, most of it. So we're not really there, we're not near equality, but there are many things to be positive about.

Women's lives should be happy, free and creative. We should all work for high self esteem, equal pay, lots of cash. I think that it's really important for women to change things. Until women have economic power there's not much hope. I think it's happening now, with each generation people evolve. As each generation comes forward and older attitudes fall by the way then things do improve.

Rosemary Lovatt

Rosemary has been a volunteer at Brighton Women's Centre for nine years doing everything from cleaning the toilets to being Company Secretary.

"I was a Councillor in London, and was principally involved in getting funding for a Women's Centre in Harlesden, which is now the Asian Women's Centre, but because I was so busy with my Council duties, I didn't have any time to get involved in it at all. Then I moved to Brighton. I had been here I suppose about a year and there was an advertisement in *The Argus* saying they were wanting to start off the new Women's Centre down at Lettice House. There was a public meeting at Brighthelm, so I went along, and they divided people up into groups of what you could do – and really the only thing I could join was the fundraising. That turned out to be quite horrendous, because the collective run down in Marlborough Place did not believe in keeping accounts, they didn't even keep cheque stubs! So we spent all these meetings in the evenings – some of us it was after work – well actually most of us, I think it was after work, and we had no basis to begin a strategy on because we just didn't know what, if anything, was

Rachael and Bella Lockey
Wonderful friends who have become our family. With much love.
From Jackie and Rosie Blackwell

Rosemary Lovatt

in the pot for starters. We spent all our time trying to sort out existing finances, not planning for raising money to help the Centre get off the ground. They got the grant from the Council, the eight thousand odd for the lease – that had gone through, but there was no backup, so to speak, so our endeavours at funding I don't think got very far in the first year at least.

I didn't know the Marlborough Place Centre – on the one occasion I went there it was a horrible dank, dripping, dark, dingy, basement and they weren't open other than a couple of times a week. They did help individual women, but worked much more as a collective where women gained strength from being part of the group, so I think the idea of the new Centre was to make it much more of a resource centre, so that not only would women gain strength from being in a collective, but also to help women who had nowhere else to go. I think the diversity helps a lot, that in theory any woman should be free to come in through the front door, and do her own thing, or do nothing at all!

I think that the success, as I can see it, apart from individual women getting whatever they need from the Centre, is the fact that so many groups have started there and then moved on, the drugs project [Oasis] is one example. From a small project it's grown into a massive organisation that has left the premises now and is providing a fully professional service to women who desperately need it.

On practical levels, we [the Women's Centre] just lack the space, so it would be excellent if we did have large premises, because then we would be able to offer all the other women's groups that have nowhere to meet, the facilities that they would like to have, rather than meeting in a draughty council office. They could come to a 'user friendly' place, which is what it should be, it should be open seven days a week for groups as well as carrying on the open sessions.

I think women do gain strength from knowing that there is something out there just for them. One thinks of all the Masonic groups, and all the men's clubs, even the old Labour Party clubs were all totally men orientated, so there is a need for somewhere that women can come and feel that they won't be looked down on, where they are treated at what ever level they come in at the door.

I can think of one woman, an Asian woman, who came into us all in tears. She'd lost her flat and her daughter had a flat and hadn't apparently been able to pay the rent, and had forgotten to tell Mum that she wasn't paying rent, so that literally she came in asking if we could find her transport to take her back up to relatives in London. We didn't at that

Rosemary Lovatt

moment know anybody with a van who would do it for free, so I was coming and going between the Centre, seeing what we could do, and just round the corner from the Centre over a shop, somebody had stuck a notice saying Flat to Let, so I thought, 'ooh, I don't know, it's worth a try'. I banged on the door and the chap said, yes, it was vacant and they could move in so long as they had got the month's deposit. So, I asked the woman if there was any chance of her scraping up the deposit – absolutely no money in their pockets – her or her daughter. So I went back to him and said, 'No they can't afford the deposit'. And he said, 'That's alright, I'll take it on the word of the Women's Centre'. So we've had good things like that, where occasionally the opposite sex has recognised our existence and done good things!

Karen Daniells
A kindred spirit.
From Jackie Blackwell

Sue Winter

Sue came to Brighton about 22 years ago and liked it because it was small and by the sea, with lots of arts and women's things happening.

" My sister was living in a feminist house and they told us about women's meetings and I went to this huge women's liberation meeting, in my little high heels, and my thick make up, and they were all in dungarees! These incredibly powerful, dynamic, articulate and assertive women, and I thought, "Wow, I like this!". I'd always had quite feminist ideals as a young woman. Always angry about sexual abuse of women, rape. It was very vibrant there [at the meeting]. There were big arguments about socialist feminism and the separatists, very political then. Just the sense of women's power was amazing. And I'd come from patriarchal South Africa. So it was a big movement then, and Brighton was very dynamic and radical feminism was at the forefront here.

I remember a very embarrassing women's liberation march with about eight of us along the seafront! Women's discos were good fun then, and these amazing women's cabarets where all sorts of women would put on all different

Sue Winter

performances. Very butch dykes in petticoats doing Swan Lake! Very funny.

I have been around [in Brighton] for a shockingly long time. I mean 19 years ago was when I got involved. Women were definitely coming forward then. There were very many dynamic women doing very dynamic things, and they were definitely not tied to the kitchen sink. We were the second or third town to set up a women's refuge. I think when each individual woman gets involved and it becomes a part of her life, then it feels dynamic to her. I think women's assertiveness is a progressive thing. We're all a product of what went before us, those women who threw themselves in front of horses to get the vote. It makes me really angry when people don't use their vote. I was brought up in South Africa where the majority of people didn't have the vote. OK, so you may be pissed off with politics, but use your vote. I don't feel very enthralled by British mainstream politics.

We've been very fortunate in Brighton, I think Brighton was really committed to Sports Development. I got involved because I had a New Year's resolution to get fit, and I needed a job. I went down the pool and there was this woman who I recognised as a dyke around town doing some bronze medallion life-saving stuff. She said it was ActionSport, a community based sports project, and they needed more women. I was interested in the community side of it because of all the community stuff I had done in Brighton. I was not at all interested in the sports side of it. I was the kid that skived off from sport to hang out with the surfers and my best mate! But she pointed out that I swam and cycled, that was fine. They gave me the job because I could draw, this was pre-desktop publishing! So from there it was a Manpower Services project to get more people from the community involved in sport. Not people who were already involved.

They had target groups and women were one of the target groups. But it was no surprise that women weren't involved because they've got childcare commitments, what are they meant to do with their children? None of the places had crêche facilities then. It was really exciting, running sessions in communities, rather than expecting people to come to the sports centres, so we would find church halls and places and put up publicity, and slowly women got involved.

The financial [commitment] that Brighton made to the project made a big difference, because we were paid to do it. When the Manpower Services withdrew their funding from the project, most of the community sports projects folded. But Brighton Council took it on mainstream and continued to fund us.

Anne Barrett
I can't describe you to people in one paragraph, but I want to dedicate a page to you because I love you, I miss you and what's more, when I tell my own daughters about you they will feel your absence too, even though you have died and they're not even born yet.
From Robyn Simms

Sue Winter

Unfortunately Hove Council wasn't so committed to sports development. They had about four people when they were getting the funding and when the money was cut they didn't put any of their money into it. They combined their play and sport departments, and the person who got the job was doing play before they got the job, so sport in Hove really took second place. Since the amalgamation we have lost posts. That's why I'm ready to leave. It's now so big. Brighton and Hove is enormous, we go right up to far edges of Southwick, and I'm responsible for all these people.

I'd like to get back to doing some artwork. I'd like to come and sit down at the Women's Centre and see what's going on. To do something more creative, well it has been very creative, because I helped build the project up because I was here right from the start, eleven years ago now. The job has changed so much, and I have developed so much through it, and I feel that I've been very privileged to have had that opportunity to do it. If I went into it now with my lack of qualifications in sport my CV would have been chucked in the bin. I've been given a lot of opportunities.

I hope with the change of government, Labour will be a bit more 'sport for all', rather than just looking at elite sport. I think most women are not elite sports women. Most have very mixed feelings about sport, maybe because of their experiences at school and stuff. Not every woman comes in feeling confident and fine about walking into a leisure centre or gym. And older women as well, they don't want to be in that environment. They want to be in a more supportive environment. We've got an over-50s exercise to music class; an older group that do bowling and I run an older women's swimming session. Most of those women never swam, and they're in their 60s, 70s now. There's a woman who comes who's in her 80s! It doesn't just provide the exercise, it provides a social contact for women. Getting away from husbands and partners is quite important for some of them. There's more yacking going on in the pool than swimming, and that's fine! For me it's never been about competition. Fine for those women who want to get involved in that path. We can suggest joining clubs to women who discover or re-discover a love for a sport. But a lot of women just come because the kids are in the creche happy, they've got a couple of hours to let off steam and run around. Get the feelings of self-worth and autonomy, 'I'm not just a mother'.

When our outdoor pursuits co-ordinator left, the Council cut the post. That was when I decided I really had to leave. Now all those courses which we used to run, for women only,

Sue Winter

for people over 50, for people with learning disabilities, are gone. We can't offer them. We can't offer an abseiling course, climbing, canoeing. I think it's a real loss. Also everything was so subsidised. We had a five-hour creche as women went off into the countryside, and had a fabulous time. Whatever the weather!

You just have to look in the media to see that sport is so male-dominated. Sometimes I still have to justify having women-only sessions, which I find amazing. Because Brighton and Hove are very committed to equal opportunities, and we work very closely with the Women's Sports Foundation, we've been given the freedom to develop women-only stuff without having to justify it too much. Still women are under represented. The Health Education Authority's 'Active for Life' campaign, which is a national campaign, from previous research, they are still seeing that 16–25 year old women are not doing enough exercise to benefit their health. You don't have to be going to a gym, the message is half an hour a day, whether it's hoovering, walking, cycling or dancing, which is a brilliant one. I've always pushed a lot of dance in the project, which has been nice for me, because I love dance!

I see women's sports developing I hope. I think it's the pebble in the pond effect. There is a women's football team who play in Preston Park every week. They just play for fun, and there is a more serious team that play as well.

I'm not a great planner aheader! I think I'll always be cycling, I love cycling about. What I'd really like to be doing is welding and carving, I'd like to be doing some amazing sculptures. Working full-time, and I'm very committed to what I do, does take up a hell of a lot of time. And I've got child care responsibilities to a little one my ex-partner and I had. I was a surrogate mother for her because she couldn't have a child, so I've got a commitment to a six year old every Saturday, so my time is very taken up.

Jackie Blackwell
For having the courage to walk down another street.
From Kelle Kingsley

Tanya Levene

Tanya is the crêche co-ordinator and a counsellor for Brighton Women's Centre.

"I grew up in north London and came down here after I'd been to America for six months to work in a residential home for children with special needs. It was Brighton because that's where my family had all grown up and because it was residential and I could live and work there. An easy option really. That was in 1989.

I had been in Brighton nearly five years and hadn't heard of the Women's Centre. I had gone from the residential care home to supervisor of a large private nursery. I was looking to get out of that and someone said that the Centre was looking for a co-ordinator for the crêche. I applied for it and about one month later started work here and have been here ever since. We got three years' funding from Children in Need. Child care is for children aged 2–5, mainly for children living in difficult circumstances i.e. bed and breakfast, temporary accommodation, for women on the drugs project, refugees, basically anyone who needs it. 90% of our children are living at home with single

Tanya Levene

parents. We work closely with the refuge project, and with social services, we only charge £1 a session, so it's very low cost. We've got a waiting list, and have six children a session. It relies on volunteers a lot as I am the only paid worker and to have six children I need one if not two volunteers per session. So that's an onward struggle. As far as the children are concerned they come flooding in. I also trained as a counsellor and started working for the Centre as one of the therapists over three years ago.

The Brighton Women's Centre offers a safe space for people to come into. The idea of having a women's space is a very good one. The information that's available is good, but we rely a lot on external people giving it to us. I feel that the Brighton Women's Centre will always go on because I think that there will always be women that have got enough energy and enthusiasm to keep it going. I think that it will have to change in its context and broaden its views. How well run it is, how well advertised it is, what services it offers etc, is at a crunch point where it's either going to go, 'yeah this is it we're going to expand, it's going to be brilliant' or it's going to continue with 'we may do this, we may do that, we haven't got enough space, we haven't got enough money etc, etc'. I think that it's quite an important time for the Brighton Women's Centre at the moment.

The Centre is presently for any woman who wants to use it. The stigma that the Brighton Women's Centre has got is basically 'women in need' – people tend to use it if they've got a problem, if they need something. It's used slightly for social reasons but that tends to be more for the out-of-towners who come in to try to meet new people or new to Brighton and it doesn't surprise me to hear that most of Brighton hasn't heard of it. I was here for five years, actively in the women's and gay scene and still hadn't heard of it. Even if I had heard of it would I have used it anyway? Because again, it's that sort of thing, it's for women in need, lottery money is for people on poverty level, so why would someone whose life is going on fine want to come in and use the welfare rights, or legal advice or counselling, which is all at very low cost? So yes, it's open to all women and yet in some ways it's not as well. What we do here is really biased at people that haven't got money, and I think that people who have got money feel guilty for using those spaces up or just think 'it's not for me, I'll pay, or find better quality elsewhere' – this image needs to change.

I've been to a couple of Women's Centres in America and one in particular in Kentucky; it was the most amazing place, women from every age were there, women from different economic backgrounds, a whole range were there, from not having a job to the top lawyers and it was just brilliant. It was relaxing, it was

Bella Lockey
From seed to flower. A wonder to behold.
Rachael Lockey

Tanya Levene

friendly, welcoming and it had everything that you could ever want, at your finger tips. They had more money I'd imagine. Everything was computerised, and 'please stay for a cup of tea we'd like to talk to you'. It was much broader, much wider, it was sort of 'it's for you – you can use it, it doesn't matter who you are' and people went in just to talk to people, just to chill out in their lunch break, to eat their sandwiches, they had a café there which therefore encouraged more women in but it was brilliant and that would be my ideal of where I'd like to go or how I'd like to see the Brighton Women's Centre going to. I think that we've got a lot to learn from other countries, but you've seen ones in Canada, I've seen ones in America, so the information is actually within the Centre, the ideas, the ideals, even possibly the enthusiasm is here as well but it's that motivation to actually get that happening, to get that money in. There is no reason why we couldn't be like that.

I actually am not sure how I feel about an all-women environment. I can see the potential in it, I can see the beauty in it, there is a need for it, but the need of it is usually for vulnerable women and we're back to where we started, that's where the need is. There is a gap for it and it could be very significant and very good. I would back an all women environment, even if I didn't want to spend all my time in there.

There are so many women's organisations, Rape Crisis, Survivors Network, and loads of smaller women's groups and I think I'd like to see that all under one roof at a women's centre.

I'd like all the people here funded. I am very for people getting paid for the work that they are doing and if they can't get paid for the actual work, then certainly, extensive child care costs. I am 100% behind training, I did have a problem when I first started here that people didn't have training, and I pushed for that over the years, although it's not really my role to do that. It's changed now, but at the time it was the only voluntary organisation that I knew where people were allowed straight in off the streets and then allowed to talk to vulnerable women on the phone, allowed to open the doors to people, without any form of training at all. I was quite gobsmacked by all of that. It's changed now and people do get training though I'd like to see a structured six-week training and then shadowing and then when they have passed that, allowed loose – if you like – on the community. There would be no reason why we couldn't do outreach work as well as within the Centre.

It's just as important for us to go around to the estates as it is to go around to Dyke Road, to get a balance. One of my first conversations at the Centre, was there was a group of seven or eight women talking about hysterectomies and I said 'that's not a problem, whip all mine out, stop me having periods, take the whole lot' and these women just stared at me, like I was completely wrong, and I thought I'm not like these people because I don't count my womb as my womanhood. After that I thought I'll just shut up. It wasn't fitting in with what they wanted to hear then. That reiterated that sort of women fighting, we've all got shaved heads, we're all radical, we're all right on and we're all going to worship our menstrual blood each month which isn't how it is for the majority of people, but it's getting that across. I'm not sure how you do that.

There's been so much ups and downs since I've been here, the first uproar I had when I came here was the fact that I was being paid, people didn't think that I should be paid for my role and I was the first paid worker within the Centre and I got loads of abuse and hassle because of the fact that I was being paid. That was my first biggie.

The biggest challenge for me would have to be the big transgender, transsexual debate. After reading that they [Brighton Women's Centre] doesn't allow transsexuals into the building, I campaigned and formed a group to change this policy. It went to two general annual meetings to be voted on. So that was my main campaign within my work as I felt exceptionally strongly about that.

That was a big change for the Centre as a lot of the older rota workers had left and a lot of new rota workers were coming in. I've seen that happen two or three times every 18 months. You obviously get the stream of people who have been here since the year dot, but there tends to be quite a high turn over when something big comes up. Which I guess is only natural when people aren't getting paid or not being valued for what they're doing and if they don't like it they are going to leave, whereas I was getting paid for it, so it was worth me staying here and campaigning for a change.

Overall I think that it has been [a positive thing], I've met some good people, I've learned a hell of a lot from just talking to different women who I probably wouldn't have had that contact with under normal circumstances. I was brought up as an orthodox Jew, in a very middle class area, went to a private all girls school – a convent school, odd for a Jewish person. I was very sheltered and moving down to Brighton and working in the Brighton Women's Centre I've learnt huge amounts but I think that it's very easy then to fall into this sort of idea that the women that I am meeting now are the majority, it's just gone from one extreme to the other for me. It's now time for me to assess my role in and out of the Centre and look forward to big changes in the near future.

Tanya Levene

Jackie Blackwell
An inspiration and a beauty. We have journeyed along now for many years. Near or far, you are always in sight. Thank you.
From Poppy Lockey

Vicki Brown

**Vicki is an accountant, born in 1965 in Portslade.
She moved to Brighton when she was three years old.**

"I was brought up at home with parents until my dad left when I was five. I went to Brighton and Hove High School when I was five and my dad left home two days after my fifth birthday. I left the High School when I was seven and went to Stanford Road, which was a bit of a culture shock having been to an all-girls school, to going to this school round the corner. Someone thought I was a boy! I was wearing jeans and a jean jacket with my pony tail tucked down the back of my jacket. I loved it there; I learnt to swim, I went dancing.

After my dad left, my mum worked nights as a nurse, so my grandmother brought me up. She lived with us. She was about 70 when I was five. She took me to school, took me dancing, took me to the paddling pool in the summer.

I went back to the High School when I was 12 It was slightly bizarre. It gave me a distorted perception of men. I didn't see any boys and so I thought they were something magical instead of something vile, which I'm sure I would have done if I'd gone to a

Vicki Brown

mixed school. We all had a crush on the Advance Laundry man who used to come and clean the towels in the toilet! There were no other men at school and I lived at home with my mother, my sister and my grandmother. We did have male lodgers, but they and all other males were deemed to be unimportant.

I had no knowledge of football or other male-dominated sports. Everything was female, which was nice in a way – I don't look at that as being a bad part of growing up.

My mum actively encouraged me not to have children. I was brought up with the sense that we were a burden to her. I was born when my mother was 23, I'm one of three daughters of different fathers. I was the second child. Myself and my sister were children that she didn't want. Not that she ever said she didn't love us, but there was no disguising the fact that she didn't want us. She wasn't a particularly doting, maternal type of woman. I never felt unloved or badly treated as a child, but I did feel like having children was not a great thing to do.

Mum was originally a nurse and a midwife and became a health visitor. Her work was all-encompassing. We had people's children coming to stay and we would cook meals for people who couldn't cook for themselves. We were dispatched as kids to do things for other people; going out in the middle of the night delivering money to people for their meters!

My dad lived in Brighton until I was about 14. He was gay and had a long-term relationship. They were what I call 'stately homosexuals'! They lived down by the station in a little two-bedroom house, which he had made into a bijou palace and lived a luxurious life really!

I'm glad I'm a woman, I wouldn't want to be a man because I think they're narrow. Women are much broader and versatile, multi-talented. I'm very proud to be a woman. I don't feel there's anything I can't achieve because I am a woman. I think sexism exists, but not in things that are really important. I've had it at work, but if I say, 'that's sexist', then they stop. When I challenged my workplace, they changed their policy.

It's acceptable for women to work and you don't have to stay at home anymore. I feel like I go to work because I have every right to work. But if we stop pushing it will just revert. I think a lot of men don't like women being powerful and strong, they find it frightening. It's important to carry on and show young women what they can do.

I want women to be free to do what they want to do, because they are good at it and not because they have to do it.

I think the best thing about being a woman is the honesty, having really good friendships, knowing I can survive. I feel that comes from being a woman.

Lynne Fox
Tenacious adventurer.
From Tom and Kelle

Brighton Women's Centre

5.74
Inaugural meeting
A re-reading of the aims was called for and in the resulting discussion it was agreed to amend them as follows: The word 'lesbian' be replaced by 'sexual problems', that in the list of additional groups, Gay Women and Women's Liberation Movement should be added.

12.74
If anyone sees a carpet for £1 or less – buy it!!

74
Many women are freaked about lesbianism. No-one should deny their feminism or lesbianism.

11.74
Rota is not full. Supposed to be at least 2 people. If you are signed up you must turn up.

9.76
Since there were so many women at this meeting we decided to possibly go to the Good Companions, but Sandy thought it would be a good idea to go to the Marlborough since the people there are friendly.

9.76
Brighton Gay Alliance are looking at opening a gay community centre in Brighton. A building was recently squatted for one day. There was some concern that the gay community squat would jeopardise the Women's Centre future, but no-one felt it would.

10.76
Alison totalled up spending of £505.80 last year.

5.76
The objective of the Centre was to raise the standing of women in society.

Brighton Women's Liberation (BWL) group had been meeting since the late 60s, and the idea of a Women's Centre was discussed as early as 1969. The idea took root in the minds of the members of BWL, who were setting up a publication entitled *A Woman's Place*. In the third issue (June 1973), the need for a woman-only space was set out in an article which appealed for information about possible sites. Even at this stage, it was envisaged that the centre would perform a variety of roles. The article expressed that,

> 'the space for a women's centre is not lacking and neither is the need. Women must have an alternative to the dead-end solutions now available. It's not enough to have stop-gap measures which help only for the moment but don't change the basic situation. And women can change their own situation, by helping each other, by talking, by trusting. A women's centre could fulfil many of a woman's needs. We could come there just to be, to end the isolation of our homes. We could try, in an atmosphere of support, to question and answer the reasons for our oppression. Children would not be unwelcome guests. Most important, we would not be forced to remain in or return to degrading circumstances.'

Although a large number of empty council properties were known to exist, the Council denied it. Squatting in one of these properties was considered, but the precariousness and impossibility of publicising such a centre ruled this out. A potential benefactor was also found to be unsuitable, as she was only prepared to give money for a cottage industry scheme.

In April 1974, a community café, Open Café, offered a room to the Working Association of Mothers (WAM), members of which were also involved in BWL. The women decided to use this opportunity as a pilot run of the Women's Centre, and they staffed the project by rota. The prototype Centre proved popular, and acquired many of the women who would become regular users in the future at this time. However, given its temporary nature, there was no phone, and no advertising of services. During this time, the women heard from a community worker that there were some properties in Buckingham Road being offered to community projects on a temporary basis. Inspired by this news, the women galvanised their support for a Centre into a special committee. The Brighton Women's Centre Committee (BWCC) was made up of members from WLM, WAM, WILPF (Women's International League for Peace and Freedom), the National Childbirth Trust, local women, and women studying at Sussex University. They met for the first time on 23 May, 1974. Special interest groups were established to take care of proposals for finance, information, education, a library and a playgroup.

The property in Buckingham Road was a council-owned building that used to be a maternity hospital. Thirty women attended the Council meeting in Lewes on June 21st, 1974 to decide its fate. The Council had the place earmarked for a special needs school, but they were undecided whether to pull the building down, or to renovate. In the meantime, however, it was voted that the BWCC could have the place for one year, with a grant of £6,000 for renovation. The Council pledged to help find new premises after the year, or to extend the tenancy further if possible.

It is thought that there were a number of factors operating to swing the vote in favour of the BWCC. East Sussex County Council were aware that their public image would be improved by approving more community projects than they had in recent years, and women's centres were opening all over the country. It appears that there was some confusion in the Councillors' minds over the distinction between the BWCC and another Committee which was active in lobbying for a Women's Aid Centre to provide a refuge for battered women. The other Committee had given the Council a great deal of information about their project, and their case was discussed before the BWCC's at the meeting. It is thought that the confusion might have led to the two being treated as one item. A questionnaire sent to the voters after the decision had been finalised suggests that this confusion operated in BWCC's favour. Women's Aid Centres were very much on the national political agenda at the time.

The timing was favourable, as the Squatters' Movement had risen, and the prospect of a voluntary organisation occupying space in a controlled way was more agreeable. In addition, the Women's Liberation Movement was getting a broader, less stereotyped image. Some of the women on the BWCC believed that the WAM members impressed the Council with their respectable appearances and their focus on practical matters,

7.79
Must shut, and slam shut, fridge door, and put chair in front of it.

2.80
Demo in London against Corrie Bill – Coaches 2.30pm from St Peters.

2.80
All night vigil to commemorate women who've died from back street abortions.

3.80
Couple of phone calls. Nobody loves G. today. P. was late but nobody smacked her botty 'cos she'd had a hard day, poor lass.

9.80
State of the Women's Centre. Please could we keep the cups clean and empty ashtrays, tidy the desk and empty the rubbish.

1.80
Demo. This morning against the closing of the New Sussex Women's hospital was poorly supported – only about 30 demonstrators and most of the nurses. Ah well, apathy rules O ...

4.80
I knew Wendy would see the light about the t-shirts – I think it's a great idea – free expression for a cause etc! Charlotte finished knitting her jumper, we read various Newsletters, ate cheese and Mars bars and discussed lesbian mothers, communal child care, contraception and why newsletters should be women only.

4.80
Been chatting about marriage etc and getting depressed about it (joke!?) I'm nearly 24 and not one single offer yet. I'll be on the shelf soon!!

8.81
No phone calls or visits of any description. We thought it might be a good idea to transfer the Women's Centre to the beach!

5.??
Woman was recommended by sales assistant in Boots who – in reply to her request for a pregnancy test kit- said she shouldn't waste £5 but go to the Women's Centre! (They're all trying to sneak off early but I'm barricading the door!!)

8.81
I stupidly cleaned the loo again!

2.81
Wish we had 2 rooms as this could have been a time when privacy would have helped. A woman was in the middle of talking rather shyly about contraception.

3.81
I was glad I was here to talk to her – had a long chat about being single with a child etc. She seemed quite strong about it and she said she felt much better having talked to me!! Sometimes we are helpful maybe!!

8.81
Rather a non-day. I wrote a letter to Brighton Swimming Pool manager re lack of facilities for women and children. How efficient!!

10.81
Dorothy and her mum came in and left a pumpkin.

12.83
We've discussed the total lack of filing method in this room and have decided we need a filing day – 11am 18/12 is filing day. Every woman, every day, should file please.

1.84
About men coming to the door, phoning up etc. We should tell them to fuck off.

12.85
More effort should be made to make new women feel welcome to the centre. I've met a couple of women who could have done with some friendly help and advice and did not find it at the Women's Centre.

such as offering babysitting services. Two men on the Social Services Committee, Chris Miller and Denis Allen, liaised extensively with the BWCC throughout their mission, and were instrumental in persuading the Councillors that the proposed Women's Centre would reduce the work load of social workers and Brighton's Citizens' Advice Bureau.

BWCC were given the house on Buckingham Road and set about renovating it. The Centre opened in November 1974. The Women's Aid Centre had the premises next door, with a passageway at the rear of the house linking the two. This was useful, as many of the women who needed the refuge first called in at the Women's Centre.

The Centre was open every day and some evenings, and became well used by a wide range of women, some of whom had been referred by Social Services. (Some members of the group rather resented being relied upon to compensate for the Social Services shortcomings. This is a problem even at the present day.) The Women's Centre provided an invaluable playgroup facility, which was heavily used, and a free pregnancy testing service, in which all the volunteers were trained, and which continues to be one of the most popular services offered by the Women's Centre. Occasional women's parties and jumble sales were held. Many groups (e.g. a health group, a psychiatry group and a co-counselling group) welcomed the opportunity to sever their reliance on pub rooms and other peoples' equipment, and met at the Centre in the evenings. This was all despite the fact that the Centre was outside of Brighton's main hub of activity and was freezing cold.

The Women's Centre was run by volunteers, primarily from the original committee, although the members of WAM had left after an argument about whether men should be allowed access to the Centre. The vote decided against this, as it was felt that a women-only space was needed, and that male access would endanger the safety of the women in the refuge next door. Another problem involved the education group, which set up projects without researching the needs of the local community.

A principal member of the BWCC was made homeless in 1975, and she moved into the Centre. Initially, this seemed like a good way to improve the security of the building, but it was soon discovered that other volunteers were relying on her expertise now that she had so much familiarity with the Centre's role. Many volunteers began to be concerned that there was a growing elitism in the Centre, and this forced her to leave in Summer 1975.

Despite the original tenancy being a year, the Centre did not have to leave until June 1976. The efforts to find new premises were in vain, and the group was forced to settle for a flat in Moulsecoomb which belonged to a sympathetic Councillor. The flat proved to be impractical, as it was a long way from the town, and the Centre dwindled. Pregnancy testing was the only benefit the Centre could offer.

In November 1976 a room in the Resource Centre was found, although it was shared with the boy scouts and was very cramped and cold. At first there was no phone, which scuppered efforts to re-establish advice on housing and welfare. Later, the Centre was given its own tiny room in the building, this time with a telephone but without toilet facilities. This room used up all of the Council grant in rent, and meant that the services on offer could not be effectively publicised.

The trail of the research in to the history of the Brighton Women's Centre goes a little cold at this point. We know that the Centre was also at Marlborough Place and in the Richmond area, eventually settling at Lettice House, 10 St George's Mews, in 1989, but little was uncovered about the years between '76 and '89, although there are poignant moments recorded in some of the women's testaments.

An arsonist caused £6,000 worth of damage to the Centre in 1994 and the Centre got its first paid co-ordinator in 1997, thanks to funding from the National Lottery.

The Centre is home to the Toybox Crêche, the Launch project and Taking Liberties Festival. It also plays host to women's groups, offering them a low cost and central meeting space. Over the last twenty-five years, hundreds – if not thousands – of women have freely given their time to the Brighton Women's Centre to ensure that it has remained open, in one way or another. Last year alone over four thousand women walked through the door of the Centre to use its services. The Centre remains at Lettice House and the ten year lease runs out this year.

5.86
Please don't give strange women my phone number.

5.87
Woman came down for pregnancy test – positive. She was so happy she kissed me!

7.88
We're concerned that few rota workers are actually turning up for rota or meetings. A few women feel like they are carrying the centre and it's not on. We're writing to all rota workers asking them to fulfill their commitment.

8.88
Woman came in very depressed. Gave her some rescue remedy and talked to her. H. is going to make up some flower remedies for her. B. is arranging for her to see a hypnotherapist. She seemed to feel a bit better.

10.94
Playgroup had a lot of children today, but not enough helpers. There could be trouble unless more people come and help- what about women with no children giving a hand and giving mothers a rest?

11.94
Mrs (?) came in, conducting a survey for East Sussex County Council. Thought the centre was still a hospital. I told her it was a day centre for women, run by women – she was not interested.

12.94 (Log book)
I took the bottles back to the off licence. 56p went to the tea money and 1 bottle of cider to me and L.

Brighton Oasis Project

It is thanks to the Women's Centre that Brighton Oasis Project exists. If it had not been for their support in letting us use their premises and creche in 1993 to establish a support group for women drug users and their children, Brighton Oasis Project would never have got off the ground. We continued to use their premises for five years, until we finally moved into our own building in 1998. We are now near neighbours, and continue our close relationship, recommending their services to many of our clients.

We have a Day Programme which runs for twelve weeks, providing breakfast and lunch daily, as well as a range of therapeutic, skill-enhancing and craft based sessions. The aim of the Day Programme is to give recently drug-free women and those on prescriptions the opportunity to take stock of their lives and acquire new skills to enable them to go forward.

We also offer short or long-term counselling with women counsellors to women who are drug free. Our pregnancy liaison worker, a trained midwife, is available at the project and other venues to discuss sexual health, contraception, pregnancy and parenting.

We offer an informal support group open to men and women concerned about Hep C which meets on the last Tuesday of the month between 7.30pm and 8.30pm.

We have creche facilities available in support of all our services except for the Hep C support group.

Women who come to Brighton Oasis Project are asked to respect the following ground rules:

- No drugs allowed on the premises
- No violence, either verbal or physical
- No racial or sexual harassment
- Do not come in stoned

Confidentiality
Brighton Oasis Project offers a confidential service. Confidentiality will be broken, however, if there are concerns about the welfare of a child or fears that a woman may commit suicide. Any concerns will be discussed with the woman first. You may ask to see our confidentiality policy.

Outreach
Our outreach workers run a drop in for young women at Brighton Oasis Project on Wednesdays between 4.30 and 6.00pm

Contacts
Helpline Monday to Friday 10am to 5pm and 24 hour answerphone on 696970.

Brighton Oasis Project
22 Richmond Place
Brighton
BN2 2NA
01273 696970

The Launch Project

The Launch Project was established in 1996 with funding from Brighton and Hove Council's Single Regeneration Budget and run through the Brighton Women's Centre. It aims to improve the employment prospects of local women through training and/or education coupled with work experience placements.

The project has been designed specifically to help women who might find it difficult to attend mainstream college courses and who need extra support to help them through a period of training and work experience. Unemployed women in receipt of Job Seekers Allowance, Income Support, Family Credit or Disability/Incapacity Allowance are all eligible for a place on the project. Priority will be given to women living in central Brighton.

On joining the project, women attend an eight week certificated induction programme designed and delivered by Sussex Careers Service. The programme incorporates career guidance with confidence building and personal development training, and aims to assist women in setting personal goals. The women are helped to identify the qualifications they need to work towards achieving their career or job-related goals. At the end of the programme, the vast majority of women will have chosen a qualification to work towards and will be ready to enrol at one of the local Colleges of Further Education during which time they will continue to receive assistance and support from the project.

A wide range of services is available to all the women during their time on the project (which might be as long as two years depending on the qualification they are working towards). These include support to find and pay for suitable childcare, financial support to cover the cost of college fees and necessary books and materials, personal counselling, welfare rights, legal and health advice and regular support group meetings.

Several employment related services are also offered: help with identifying a suitable and appropriate work placement in either the voluntary or private sector, help with CVs, writing job applications and interview techniques.

Launch Project
Brighton Women's Centre
10 St George's Mews
Brighton BN1 4EU
01273 600526

Toy Box Creche

The Women's Centre has always aimed to provide a safe space for children. Up until October 1993 it was staffed by volunteers, or individual paid workers from groups who were using the Centre. In October 1993 the Centre was awarded three years' funding from Children in Need to set up creche provision for children aged 2–5 years. The target group was children living in difficult circumstances e.g. bed and breakfast and temporary accommodation.

A Co-ordinator was employed, and the creche was checked by the fire department and the Health and Safety board. It was painted, policies written, toys, books and equipment bought. It was opened successfully in November 1993.

Most of the children initially were referred from Social Services, the Unemployed Centre, Women's Refuge Project, the Bed and Breakfast Support Group and Family Centres.

Although we still take referrals most of the users hear about the creche from word of mouth. Parents/carers do not need to stay on the premises but are welcome to use the Centre's facilities if they choose to.

The creche is run by the Co-ordinator and relies strongly on volunteers. We are currently funded by a number of different organisations and charities including The Gatsby Charitable Foundation, The Community of the Blessed Virgin Mary, Brighton and Hove Council, The National Lottery, the Launch Project, Lloyds, TSB, Family Assurance, Somerfield Community Charity and Communication and Workers Union.

The creche takes a maximum of 6 children per session, and each session lasts $2^{1}/_{2}$ hours. We are currently full and have a waiting list.

For further details please contact Tanya at:

Toy Box Creche
Brighton Women's Centre
10 St George's Mews
Brighton
BN1 4EU
01273 600526

The Women's Refuge Project

The Women's Refuge Project was formed in January 1994 by a group of women's organisations including the Brighton Women's Centre. It has an elected Management Committee and paid professional staff. The Project offers advice and support to women and children who have experienced domestic violence, and refuge if they need it. It funds a Children and Young People's Service, a housing support service and consultancy and training service. The Project also undertakes to improve awareness of domestic violence in the community. It is run by women for the benefit of all women and children whatever their abilities, age, class, race, religion or sexuality. The Project works primarily with women and children from the local area, though increasingly we are getting referrals both from around the country and abroad.

The first five staff were appointed to the Project in August 1994 to set up a Refuge and community based Outreach Service.

Initially the Outreach Service was based in the Brighton Women's Centre, within the first year of 1995/1996 a total of 881 women were referred to the Outreach Service. These women had a total of 938 dependant children living with them. Given the large numbers of referrals it soon became evident that the project would have to move to its own premises. In 1996 it identified a suitable building and moved on with feelings of excitement, mixed with sadness, at leaving the Centre.

The work of the Refuge Project continues to be supported by the Brighton Women's Centre. It now has 17 staff who span different areas of the Project's work. This may appear to be a relatively large number of staff, however it is put into proportion when we recall that in the year 1997–98 the Project received referrals of 1,692 women and 1,835 children. This year the project expects to receive referrals of over 2,000 women with more than 2,000 children.

The Project retains a special link with the Brighton Women's Centre. Its Director Jean Calder said:

> The Women's Centre accommodated the Outreach Service in its first year, Sue [Phipps] and I shared a general office with all rota workers and any woman who needed to use the computer. We had exclusive use of an interview room for three mornings a week.

Our presence must have terribly inconvenienced the Centre but no one ever complained. We stayed there a year, set up the helpline, built the service and eventually moved on. We could not have done it without the Centre's support and help. We will always be grateful for that and really value the continuing strong relationship we have with the Centre.

Our time at the Women's Centre was a really positive period. We benefited from being based in an already well established local community setting. We were able to link into Projects already running from the Centre such as the Toy Box Crèche and counselling service. It was invaluable having Women's Centre rota workers around who supported our work in many different ways. We really missed being there when it was time to move out to our own premises.

Women's Refuge Project
P.O.Box 889
Brighton
01273 622822

Quotes about the Women's Centre

"Last year we started on the LAUNCH Project. We learning language, because the main problem we get is language. I feel I am not comfortable with the language and with communication with people because English people different. I am not comfortable anyway. If you don't know even the language, you can't do it, you can't do the courses, specific courses. Julia is funding the money for registration..."
Faduma

"We've been coming to the Centre for two years now. I wouldn't do what I am doing now if Julia wasn't here. I might be still behind, left behind laughing or go back to McDonald's" **Rakma**

"I found the creche at the Women's Centre invaluable, it meant I could have a safe place to leave my children while I could grab a few hours just for myself, to swim, to meet with friends for coffee or just look around the shops." **Linda White**

"I think I'd like a Women's Centre that served food, where you could go along and have something to eat. I think that very often, sitting in a situation where you are eating is a very good way of meeting other women and talking and I think a lot of the valuable work of the Brighton Women's Centre is done informally and I think there is nothing like food to facilitate that."
Maria

"I think the Brighton Women's Centre provides a very useful space for women to go to, a safe space, a welcoming space and it provides a lot of information, which is one of the main things and it's a kind of supportive environment. I've done a few pregnancy tests on women and I think its been nice that they've been able to stay in the Centre afterwards and talk through how they feel about the result and they're not just sent out of the door." **Maria**

"I thought if we were going to have any coherent movement at all, communication was really important. So I was involved in the newsletter and did rota."
Sue Winter

"I think it's really nice to have somewhere to find out what's going on, especially if you're new in town" **Sue Winter**

"I remember going quite recently and being impressed by how much it has evolved."
Sue Winter

"I think women's commitment is amazing but if you can get paid for the work then that's brilliant. It would be great to have more than one worker really."
Sue Winter

"I did go down to see the Solicitor for some free legal advice … And for the LAUNCH Project, but they had a waiting list."
Alanna Price

"I fundamentally believe in that through being in lots of different work situations and social situations where if it is mixed company then the majority of the vocal space is taken up by men and that the needs of women are not a priority." **Bunty Dann**

"I work with young women among girl's groups, and its because in the youth club set up they tend to get turfed to the peripheries, it is very easy for them to be standing on the edges." **Bunty Dann**

"If there were more women I thought I could identify with then it might be more welcoming. The Women's Centre is quite unwelcoming to professional women."
Vicki Brown

"It seems to be everything is pushing us to move, whether its over the edge of the cliff or not I don't know."
Liz Williams

"It's taught me a lot about the voluntary sector and about dealing with people."
Liz Williams

"I still think that there's a need for Women Only space all over the place… I feel very strongly that women need to always, always do things on their own."
Jen Murray

"Sisterly, sisterhood was a word that gradually tailed off in the use as people became more cynical about the use of the word." **Jen Murray**

"I think that the Women's Centre could be more supportive of women who are out there doing things in the world. But I'm glad that the Brighton Women's Centre is there as a safe space for women only" **Polly Marshall**

"It couldn't be party political anyway because it's a charity. Political in the sense of saying don't agree with government policy … I don't see any reason why the Women's Centre shouldn't take a view on that, indeed it does, doesn't it." **Joyce Edmond-Smith**

"What I think the Women's Centre is doing very effectively is its projects. Because it's here, it's able to bring together skills and ideas and that's very useful … I used to be a rota worker. At one point I was the rota worker co-ordinator, a couple of years ago." **Joyce Edmond-Smith**

"My initial impressions of the Centre was that is was a very friendly place. I have since recommended it to people who've wanted to find out more about support groups for women." **Emma**

"The preconceptions are probably that it is full of lesbians, and totally anti-man. But it actually felt just like a totally supportive women's atmosphere." **Emma**

"I think the value in having a women's only space allows women to focus on their needs rather than maybe rather than thinking that their needs are secondary in some way to men's." **Emma**

"The thing about having children to me was that I wanted to look after them, I didn't really want to work, and I was lucky enough not to have to. I don't really know how people like my mother just managed to have two children, but they did – but birth control made it much easier for women to control their security which I think is terribly important" **Patti**

I just think men and women are two such totally different creatures, I think there's so many things which make people different to each other. I mean men aren't equal either, you know, where you were born, what advantages did you have? How clever you are, how lucky you are, all sorts of things. So I think it's very difficult to say there's equality. I think there is a struggle … but women certainly don't have the same deal out of life as men, for one thing having children. **Patti**

"The Centre is very friendly, I mean everyone is welcome there, just pop in for a cup of tea and see what you think basically."
Emma (Ex- Rota Worker)

"A typical shift would vary quite a lot. Sometimes it would be something quite intense like a pregnancy test, if someone had an unwanted pregnancy... other times it would be really light hearted, someone would come in for a cup of coffee and a chat, so you didn't really know what to expect. That was part of what was interesting about it."
Emma (Ex-Rota Worker)

"They needed volunteers, and I just came along. It was very easy. I came with the idea that I really wanted to do something and it was easy to get involved. I did some articles for Broadsheet. I became a rota worker and I thought there's great potential here, lets do something, so I became involved with fundraising." **Geraldine**

"Young women often come in and are interested in volunteering but they want, need to be employed and then they suddenly disappear because they get jobs." **Geraldine**

About Women's Words

Kelle Kingsley and Whizz

Jackie Blackwell

Melita Dennett

Shirley West

The idea for this book came about when a small group of women got together in November 1997 to record the history of Brighton Women's Centre. We felt it was important to document this as well as provide a general view of the diversity of women's lives in spent in Brighton over the past 25 years. Women's Words has become a group in itself, with many women becoming involved in the process. It has been at times a traumatic and stressful process, but we believe it has been worthwhile. If you would like more details about Women's Words please contact us at 59 Stanmer Park Road, Brighton BN1 7JL.

Project Team

Project Co-ordinator:
Kelle Kingsley

Research:
Kelle Kingsley
Charlie Mounter
Emma Seers
Robyn Simms
Shirley West

Interviewers:
Roz Cran
Melita Dennett
Lynne Fox
Gail Hopkins
Kelle Kingsley
Charlie Mounter
Emma Seers

Transcribers:
Jackie Blackwell
Robyn Foreman
Gail Hopkins
Kelle Kingsley
Charlie Mounter
Emma Seers
Shirley West

Editing:
Jackie Blackwell
Melita Dennett

Layout and Design:
Erica Smith
Melita Dennett

Photography:
Lynne Fox

Proof Reading:
Roz Cran

Acknowledgements

Financial Support:
Hedgecock Bequest
Brighton & Hove Council
Brighton Women's Centre
Friends of Woman's Words
Sponsors of pages

Special Thanks to:
Feryal Melville
Julia Winckler
Maria Sullivan
Taking Liberties Festival
QueenSpark Books
CROW Radio Workshop
Do Tongues *for the Helen Zahavi interview*
Brighton Ourstory Project *for the Nic Fryer interview*